TAMIL

SELF-TAUGHT

(IN ROMAN CHARACTERS)

TAMIL
SELF-TAUGHT
(IN ROMAN CHARACTERS)

With English Phonetic Pronunciation

DON M. DEZ. WICKREMASINGHE

GYAN

Published by

GYAN

Gyan Publishing House
5, Ansari Road
Daryaganj, New Delhi-110002
Phone: 011-47034999, 9811692060
E-mail: books@gyanbooks.com

Distribution Network
gyanbooks.com
India, USA, Canada, UK, Australia, France

ISBN : 978-81-212-3065-0 (PB)
First Published, London, 1916

2nd Impression 2020

Printed at: Gyan Press, Delhi.

Tamil Self-Taught
Author: Don M. DEZ. Wickremasinghe

MARLBOROUGH'S SELF-TAUGHT SERIES.

Tamil Self-Taught.

(IN ROMAN CHARACTERS.)

WITH ENGLISH

PHONETIC PRONUNCIATION.

BY

Don M. de ZILVA WICKREMASINGHE, Hon. M.A. (Oxon.)

Epigraphist to the Ceylon Government;
Lecturer in Tamil and Telugu in the University of Oxford;
Author of TAMIL GRAMMAR SELF-TAUGHT.

SECOND EDITION, REVISED.

LONDON:
E. MARLBOROUGH & Co., 51, OLD BAILEY, E.C.
1911.

PREFACE.

THIS volume of Tamil is issued with a two-fold object, viz., as an independent manual of spoken Tamil, and as a supplementary and companion volume to TAMIL GRAMMAR SELF-TAUGHT (MARLBOROUGH'S *Self-Taught Series*, No. 19).

It is primarily intended to supply a working and practical knowledge of the language, for the benefit of those who have not the time or the inclination to master the grammar, and yet require to use the spoken tongue for purposes of business or pleasure. With this in view many vocabularies are supplied, carefully selected to suit the needs of the Tamil countries and classified according to subject, and also a large number of colloquial phrases and sentences of a practical character, similarly classified. Throughout these sections of the volume the pronunciation of the Tamil words is added, according to Marlborough's system of phonetics—a system which has grown out of long experience, and is of so simple a nature that, by means of it, a stranger to the language who knows English only, can read off the words at a glance and thus easily make himself understood amongst Tamil-speaking people. At the same time the GRAMMAR forms a useful book of reference on any point of construction, etc., which may arise.

To the student who has set himself to master the first volume—TAMIL GRAMMAR SELF-TAUGHT—this book offers a large amount of additional matter of an extremely useful kind. He can add largely to his stock of words by means of it, and the conversations furnish abundant material for exercise in writing and reading as well as in speaking Tamil. The English-Tamil alphabetical Vocabulary is a most useful supplement to the classified lists of words in the earlier portion of the book, and forms the counterpart of the *Tamil-English Vocabulary* supplied in the GRAMMAR.

Each of these volumes is, therefore, the complement of the other, and together they suffice to give an excellent grounding in Tamil. In view of the importance of the problems of government now engaging attention in India, it is hoped that, by facilitating the acquisition of one of the principal tongues of the Indian Empire, these books may assist in strengthening the ties which bind British and Indian fellow-subjects together.

M. DE ZILVA WICKREMASINGHE.

The Indian Institute,
Oxford, December, 1906.

CONTENTS.

CONTENTS.

TAMIL SELF-TAUGHT.

THE ALPHABET AND PRONUNCIATION.

The Tamil Alphabet contains thirty letters, viz., twelve vowels and eighteen consonants.

From these are formed 216 *syllabic* characters, which are combinations of the consonants with the vowels in which the consonantal character is in some cases slightly modified in form and has a vowel-sign joined to it.

In addition, there are a number of conventional abbreviated characters, etc., found in official documents and manuscripts. For these, the student is referred to TAMIL GRAMMAR SELF-TAUGHT—Volume No. 19 of this series, pages 13-14.

In the Tamil language there are five primary vowel sounds, viz., *a*, *i*, *u*, *e*, *o*. Each of these, however, is represented by two characters which stand for the long and the short sound of the vowel respectively, and there are in addition two characters representing the diphthongs *ai* and *au*.

There are thus twelve characters in the Tamil alphabet which stand for vowel sounds. These are used in two different ways, that is to say:

(*a*) INITIALLY, when they are represented separately by regular letters;

(*b*) MEDIALLY, or following and joined to a consonant to form a syllable, when the vowel is represented by a sign (in certain instances variable) attached to the consonantal character, excepting in the case of the vowel *a*, which is *inherent* in the consonant and not indicated by any sign, its *absence* being generally shown by a dot or a small circle over the consonant (see pages 10-11).

In the following tables—pp. 7 to 9—the initial and medial forms of the Tamil vowels are given, followed by the consonants, and to all are added their transliterative (Roman) characters, and the phonetic signs by which the Tamil sounds are represented in the third column throughout the classified Vocabularies and Conversations of which this volume chiefly consists.

On pages 10 and 11 are the syllabic characters, also in the Tamil and Roman types.

1. Vowels or *uyir-eṛuttugaḷ* ("life-letters"):—

Tamil Characters.		Transliteration.	Pronunciation.	Phonetic Signs.*
Initial.	Medial.			
அ		a†	Like *u* in *cut*, or *a* in *America*	u, ŭ
ஆ	ா, ர	ā	„ *a* in *rather* or *car*... ...	ah
இ	ி	i‡	„ *i* in *sit*	i
ஈ or ஈ	ீ	ī‡	„ *i* in *routine*, or *ee* in *meet*	ee
உ	ு, ு, ு	u	„ *u* in *put*, or *oo* in *good*... When final, it is pronounced very slightly, and often like *i*.	ŭ
ஊ	ூ, ூ, ூ, ூ	ū	„ *u* in *rule*, or *oo* in *fool*...	oo
எ	ெ	e‡	„ *e* in *elbow*	e
ஏ	ே	ē‡	„ *a* in *able*, *pane* ... ... When initial, the short and long *e* are pronounced like *ye* in *yes* and *yea* respectively	ay ye, yay
ஐ	ை, ை	ai äi	„ *ai* in *aisle*, or *ei* in *height* When final, it is invariably pronounced like *ei* in *veil*...	i ay
ஒ	ொ	o	„ *o* n *pot*	o
ஓ	ோ	ō	„ *o* in *noble*	oh
ஔ	ௌ	au	„ *ow* in *now*	ow

* The notes on pronunciation on p. 12 serve to emphasize the distinctive character of the phonetic signs.

† அ *a* before ர் *r*, ல் *l*, ள் *ḷ*, ழ் *ṛ*, ன் *ṉ*, and ண் *ṇ*, at the end of a polysyllabic word, is prononnced somewhat like *e* in *pen*.

‡ Before the cerebrals ட் *ḍ*, ண் *ṇ*, ழ் *ṛ*, ள் *ḷ*, and ற் *ṟ*, these vowels are pronounced with some modification, as a "modified vowel" (*umlaut*) in German.

2. CONSONANTS or *mey-eruttugaḷ* ("body-letters"):—

Tamil Characters.	Transliteration.	Pronunciation.	Phonetic Signs.
க்	k	Like *k* in *kite* when initial, doubled, mute, or immediately after ட் *ṭ* or ற் *ṯ* ...	k
	g	Like *g* in *regard* in all other instances ...	g, gh
	h	When intervocal, in Ceylon	h
ங்	ṅ	Like *ng* in song	ng
ச்	c	When doubled, or after ட் or ற், it has the sound of *ch* in *church*	ch
	j	After ஞ் *ñ* it is pronounced like *j*... ...	j
		In the case of words borrowed from Sanskrit, it generally retains the sound of the original letter.	
	ç	In all other instances it is between *s* in *sun* and *sh* in *short*	sh
ஞ்	ñ	Like *ny* in *Bunyan* (the Spanish *ñ*) ...	ny
		When followed by *j*, like *ng* in *sponge* ...	*ng*
ட்	ḍ	As *d* in *door*	d
	ṭ	When mute or doubled, it has the sound of *t* in *but*	t
ண்	ṇ	Cerebral* *n* uttered with the tip of the tongue turned up and drawn back so as to touch the roof of the dome of the palate	*n*
த்	t	When initial, mute, or doubled, it has a sound between that of *th* in *Thames* and *th* in *thick*	th
	d	In all other instances it is pronounced like the Latin *d*, or the English *th* in *these*	*th*
		In Sanskrit derivatives it more or less retains the sound of the original.	

* "Cerebral" indicates sounds made high up in the roof of the mouth.

Tamil Characters.	Transliteration.	Pronunciation.	Phonetic Signs.
ந்	n	Like *n* in *nut*	n
ப்	p b	Like *p* when initial, mute, or doubled ... Like *b* when intervocal ... ... (In Sanskrit derivatives it often retains the sound of the original letter.)	p b
ம்	m	As in English	m
ய்	y	do. do.	y
ர்	r	do. do.	r
ல்	l	do. do.	l
வ்	v	do. do.	v
ழ்	ṛ	A cerebral having the combined sound of *r* and soft *l*, and pronounced by turning up the tip of the tongue as far back as possible ... ... In Ceylon, however, it is pronounced like an ordinary English *l* ... ... In the Tamil country it has often the sound of the *s* in *pleasure* (the French *j*)	ry l
ள்	ḷ	A cerebral *l*	*l*
ற்	r̲ t̲	A hard, vibrating, half-palatal, half-cerebral *r* ... ... When mute or doubled, it is pronounced *t*	rr *t*
ன்	n̲	Nearly the English *n* ... ... ன்ற *n̲ra* is pronounced *ndra*	n ndra
ஃ, ஃ	ḥ	This letter is called the *āydam*, and is pronounced like *ch* in the Scotch word *loch*. It is used in poetry, when necessary for the metre	*ch*

8. The following table shows how the twelve medial-vowel signs are attached to the foregoing eighteen consonants, thereby producing 216 *syllabic* characters :—

Consonants.	Absence of dot = a	ā	i	ī	u	ū
க் k	க ka	கா kā	கி ki	கீ kī	கு ku	கூ kū
ங் ṅ	ங ṅa	ஙா ṅā	ஙி ṅi	ஙீ ṅī	ஙு ṅu	ஙூ ṅū
ச் ç	ச ça	சா çā	சி çi	சீ çī	சு çu	சூ çū
ஞ் ñ	ஞ ña	ஞா ñā	ஞி ñi	ஞீ ñī	ஞு ñu	ஞூ ñū
ட் ḍ	ட ḍa	டா ḍā	டி ḍi	டீ ḍī	டு ḍu	டூ ḍū
ண் ṇ	ண ṇa	ணா ṇā	ணி ṇi	ணீ ṇī	ணு ṇu	ணூ ṇū
த் t	த ta	தா tā	தி ti	தீ tī	து tu	தூ tū
ந் n	ந na	நா nā	நி ni	நீ nī	நு nu	நூ nū
ப் p	ப pa	பா pā	பி pi	பீ pī	பு pu	பூ pū
ம் m	ம ma	மா mā	மி mi	மீ mī	மு mu	மூ mū
ய் y	ய ya	யா yā	யி yi	யீ yī	யு yu	யூ yū
ர் r	ர ra	ரா rā	ரி ri	ரீ rī	ரு ru	ரூ rū
ல் l	ல la	லா lā	லி li	லீ lī	லு lu	லூ lū
வ் v	வ va	வா vā	வி vi	வீ vī	வு vu	வூ vū
ழ் ṛ	ழ ṛa	ழா ṛā	ழி ṛi	ழீ ṛī	ழு ṛu	ழூ ṛū
ள் ḷ	ள ḷa	ளா ḷā	ளி ḷi	ளீ ḷī	ளு ḷu	ளூ ḷū
ற் ṟ	ற ṟa	றா ṟā	றி ṟi	றீ ṟī	று ṟu	றூ ṟū
ன் ṉ	ன ṉa	னா ṉā	னி ṉi	னீ ṉī	னு ṉu	னூ ṉū

e	ē	ai	o	ō	au	Consonants.
கெ *ke*	கே *kē*	கை *kai*	கொ *ko*	கோ *kō*	கௌ *kau*	க் *k*
ஙெ *ṅe*	ஙே *ṅē*	ஙை *ṅai*	ஙொ *ṅo*	ஙோ *ṅō*	ஙௌ *ṅau*	ங் *ṅ*
செ *çe*	சே *çē*	சை *çai*	சொ *ço*	சோ *çō*	சௌ *çau*	ச் *ç*
ஞெ *ñe*	ஞே *ñē*	ஞை *ñai*	ஞொ *ño*	ஞோ *ñō*	ஞௌ *ñau*	ஞ் *ñ*
டெ *ḍe*	டே *ḍē*	டை *ḍai*	டொ *ḍo*	டோ *ḍō*	டௌ *ḍau*	ட் *ḍ*
ணெ *ṇe*	ணே *ṇē*	ணை *ṇai*	ணொ *ṇo*	ணோ *ṇō*	ணௌ *ṇau*	ண் *ṇ*
தெ *te*	தே *tē*	தை *tai*	தொ *to*	தோ *tō*	தௌ *tau*	த் *t*
நெ *ne*	நே *nē*	நை *nai*	நொ *no*	நோ *nō*	நௌ *nau*	ந் *n*
பெ *pe*	பே *pē*	பை *pai*	பொ *po*	போ *pō*	பௌ *pau*	ப் *p*
மெ *me*	மே *mē*	மை *mai*	மொ *mo*	மோ *mō*	மௌ *mau*	ம் *m*
யெ *ye*	யே *yē*	யை *yai*	யொ *yo*	யோ *yō*	யௌ *yau*	ய் *y*
ரெ *re*	ரே *rē*	ரை *rai*	ரொ *ro*	ரோ *rō*	ரௌ *rau*	ர் *r*
லெ *le*	லே *lē*	லை *lai*	லொ *lo*	லோ *lō*	லௌ *lau*	ல் *l*
வெ *ve*	வே *vē*	வை *vai*	வொ *vo*	வோ *vō*	வௌ *vau*	வ் *v*
ழெ *ṛe*	ழே *ṛē*	ழை *ṛai*	ழொ *ṛo*	ழோ *ṛō*	ழௌ *ṛau*	ழ் *ṛ*
ளெ *ḷe*	ளே *ḷē*	ளை *ḷai*	ளொ *ḷo*	ளோ *ḷō*	ளௌ *ḷau*	ள் *ḷ*
றெ *ṟe*	றே *ṟē*	றை *ṟai*	றொ *ṟo*	றோ *ṟō*	றௌ *ṟau*	ற் *ṟ*
னெ *ṉe*	னே *ṉē*	னை *ṉai*	னொ *ṉo*	னோ *ṉō*	னௌ *ṉau*	ன் *ṉ*

PRELIMINARY NOTES.

Pronunciation.—The student is recommended to master the pronunciation at the outset. The precise use and value of each phonetic sign are shown on pages 7 to 9, which should be studied carefully. The following additional explanations will be of service:—

*The principles on which Marlborough's system of phonetics is based are: (1) the employment of English characters with their ordinary pronunciation (or *one* of their sounds, where more than one), with as sparing a use as possible of diacritic signs; and (2) ONE SIGN, ONE SOUND. Where, therefore, a "sign" (i.e., letter or letters) might be variously sounded—and this applies to each of the English vowels and some of the consonants—its particular use in the scheme of phonetics should be carefully noted, and each sign must always be sounded in the same manner wherever it occurs (*one sign, one sound*); any letter or combination of letters printed in italics or with any mark added has a special use which must be learnt. Thus:—

u represents (*always and only*) the sound of *u* in *bun*, *sum*.
ŭ „ the sound of *e* in *other*, *filbert*, &c.
ū „ „ „ *u* in *pull*, or *oo* in *foot*.
oo „ „ „ *u* in *rude*, or *oo* in *boor*.
i „ „ „ *i* or *y* in *pity*.
i (ital.) „ „ „ *i* in *mine* or *I* (i.e., a diphthong).
e „ „ „ *e* in *men*, *merry*.
ay „ „ „ *a* in *able*, *pane* (i.e., a simple sound, *not diphthongized*),
ay (ital.) „ „ „ *ay* (diphthong) in *day*, *play*.
ch (ital.) „ „ „ *ch* in the Scotch word *loch*.
gh is written for *g* before *e* and *i* to preserve the hard sound of *g* as in *regard*.
ow represents the sound of *ow* in *cow*, *now*.
rr „ one strong sound, the two *r*'s not to be sounded separately.
th „ the sound of *th* in *with*, *both*.
th (ital.) „ „ „ *th* in *they*, *breathe*.

For the cerebrals *n* and *l*, also for *ng*, *ny*, and ry, see Alphabet.

Tonic Accent.—It should be noted that the first syllable of a Tamil word has, as a general rule, a fuller intonation than the remaining syllables of the word.

* This paragraph is adapted from *Tamil Grammar Self-Taught* (Marlborough's Self-Taught Series.)

VOCABULARIES.*

1. The World and its Elements.

(*Ulagam-um adaṉ pūtaṅgaḷ-um.*)

English.	Tamil (romanized).	Pronunciation.
Air	*vāyu*	vahyū
cloud	*mēgam*	maygŭm
cold	*kuḷir*	kūlir
darkness	*iruḷ*	irūl
dew	*paṉi*	puni
earth	*pūmi*	boomi
East	*kiṛakku*	ki-ryukkū
fire	*neruppu*	nerūppū
fog	*mūḍu-paṉi*	moodū-puni
hail	*ālāṅkaṭṭi*	ahlahng-kutti
heat	*çūḍu*	shoodū
light	*oḷi*	oli
lightning	*miṉṉal*	minnūl
moon	*çandiraṉ*	shunthirūn
moonlight	*nilā*	nilah
nature	*çubāvam, iyalbu*	shūbahvūm, iyulbū
North	*vaḍakku*	vudŭkkū
rain	*maṛäi*	muryay
rainbow	*vāṉa-vil*	vahnŭvil
shade	*niṛal, çāyäi*	ni-ryŭl, chahyay
shadow, reflection	*pirativimbam*	pirŭthivimbŭm
sky	*vāṉam*	vahnŭm
South	*teṟku, teṉ*	thetkū, then
sun	*çūriyaṉ*	shooriyŭn
thunder	*iḍi*	idi
water	*nīr, taṇṇīr*	neer, thunneer
West	*mēṟku, mēl*	maytkū, mayl
wind	*kāṯṯu*	kahttū

2. Land and Water. (*Nilam-um nīr-um.*)

English	Tamil	Pronunciation
Bank (of a river [or lake)	*karäi*	kuray
coast	*kaḍaṟ-karäi*	kudŭt-kuray
foam	*nuräi*	nūray
hill	*maläi*	mulay

* For the absence of ARTICLES in Tamil, and for GENDER, see *Tamil Grammar Self-Taught*, page 25.

English.	Tamil (romanized).	Pronunciation.
ice	*ur̲äi-nīr*	ūrr*ay*-neer
island	*dīvu*	*th*eevū
lake	*ēri*	(y)ayri
land	*nilam*	nilŭm
mountain	*maläi*	mul*ay*
mud	*çēr̲u*	shayrrū
plain	*veḷi*	ve*l*i
pond	*kuḷam*	kū*l*ŭm
river	*ār̲u*	ahrrū
rock	*pār̲äi, kan̲-maläi*	pahrr*ay*, kun-mul*ay*
sand	*maṇal*	mu*n*ŭl
sea	*kaḍal*	kudŭl
shore	*karäi, tīram*	kur*ay*, theerŭm
star	*tāragäi*	thahrŭ-g*ay*
storm	*puyal*	pūyŭl
stream	*nīr-ōṭṭam*	neer-ohttŭm
tank	*kuḷam, ēri*	kū*l*ŭm, (y)ayri
tide (high, low)	*ēt̲t̲am, vat̲t̲am*	(y)ay*tt*ŭm, vu*tt*ŭm
valley	*paḷḷattākku*	pu*ll*ŭth-thahkkū
water (fresh)	*nalla-taṇṇīr*	nullŭ-thu*nn*eer
— (salt)	*uppu-t-taṇṇīr*	ŭppūth-thu*nn*eer
waterfall	*aruvi*	urūvi
wave	*aläi, tiräi*	ul*ay*, thir*ay*
well	*kiṇar̲u*	ki*n*ŭrru

3. Minerals and Metals. (*Niraça-castugaḷ-um ulōgaṅgaḷ-um.*)

English.	Tamil (romanized).	Pronunciation.
Brass	*pittaḷäi*	piththŭ*lay*
bronze	*veṇgalam*	ve*n*gŭlŭm
cement	*paçäi, paṭṭu*	push*ay*, puttū
chalk	*çīmäic-cuṇṇāmbu*	sheem*ay*ch chŭ*nn*ahmbū
clay	*kaḷi-maṇ*	ku*l*i-mu*n*
coal	*kari*	kuri
copper	*çembu*	shembū
coral	*pavaḷam*	puvŭ*l*ŭm
diamond	*vajjira-maṇi, vayi-[ram*	vujjirŭ-mu*n*i, vuyirŭm
emerald	*maragadam*	murŭgŭ*th*ŭm
glass	*kaṇṇāḍi*	ku*nn*ahdi
gold	*pon̲, taṅgam*	pon, thung-gŭm
granite	*karuṅ-gal*	kurŭng-gul
gravel	*parumaṇal*	purŭ-mu*n*ŭl

English.	Tamil (romanized).	Pronunciation.
iron	*irumbu*	irūmbū
lead	*īyam*	eeyum
lime	*çuṇṇāmbu*	shū*nn*ahmbū
marble	*veṇ-gal, māk-kal*	ve*n*-gul, mahk-kul
mercury	*iraçam*	irushūm
pearl	*muttu*	mūttū
plumbago	*kār-īyam*	kahr-eeyūm
ruby	*māṇikkam*	mah*n*ikkūm
sapphire	*nīla-maṇi*	neela-mu*n*i
silver	*veḷḷi*	ve*ll*i
soda	*uvar-maṇ*	ūvūr-mu*n*
steel	*eḥku, urukku*	ec*h*kū, ūrūkkū
stone	*kal*	kul
tin	*tagaram*	thugūrūm

4. Animals, Birds, Fishes and Insects.

(*Mirugam, patci, mīṉ, pūcci ādigaḷ.*)

English.	Tamil (romanized).	Pronunciation.
Animal	*mirugam*	mirūghūm
ant	*eṟumbu*	(y)errūmbū
barking	*kuläippu*	kūl*ay*ppū
bear	*karaḍi*	kurūdi
bird	*kuruvi, paṟavāi*	kūrūvi, purrūv*ay*
bleating	*kadaṟudal*	ku*th*ūrrū*th*ūl
braying	*kaṉäippu*	kun*ay*ppū
bull	*erudu, kāḷäi*	(y)erū*th*ū, kah*lay*
a calf	*kaṉṟu*	kundrū
cat	*pūṉäi*	poon*ay*
cattle	*āḍumāḍu*	ahdūmahdū
cock	*çēval, kōṟi*	shayvūl, koh-ryi
cow	*paçu, māḍu*	pushū, mahdū
crab	*naṇḍu*	nu*n*dū
crow	*kākkäi*	kahkk*ay*
dog	*nāy*	nahy
donkey	*kaṟudäi*	ku-ryū*thay*
duck	*tārā*	thahrah
eagle	*kaṟugu*	ku-ryūgū
eel	*malaṅgu*	mulūng-gū
elephant	*āṉäi*	(y)ahn*ay*
feather	*iṟagu*	irrūgū
fish	*mīṉ*	meen

English.	Tamil (romanized).	Pronunciation.
fox	*nari*	nuri
goat	*veḷḷāḍu*	ve*ll*ahdū
he-goat	*veḷḷāṭṭuk-kaḍā*	ve*ll*ahttūkkudah
she-goat	*veḷḷāṭṭu-maṟi*	ve*ll*ahttū-murri
goose	*vāttu, perun-tārā*	vahththu, perūn-thahrah
hair	*mayir*	muyir
hare	*muçal*	mūshŭl
hen	*peṭṭāik-kōṟi*	pett*ay*kkoh-ryi
herd	*mandāi*	mun*thay*
hoof	*kuḷambu, kuram*	kū*l*ŭmbū, kūrūm
horn	*kombu, kōḍu*	kombū, kohdū
horse	*kudirāi*	kū*th*ir*ay*
lamb	*āṭṭukkuṭṭi*	ahttūkkūtti
lion	*çiṅgam*	shing-gŭm
mane	*piḍar-mayir*	pidŭr-muyir
monkey	*kuraṅgu*	kūrŭng-gū
mosquito	*koçugu*	koshū-gū
mouse	*çuṇḍ'eli*	shū*n*deli
mule	*kōvēṟu-kaṛudāi*	kohvayrrū-kuryu*thay*
mungoose	*kīri*	keeri
owl	*āndāi*	ahn*thay*
ox	*māḍu, erudu*	mahdū, erū*th*ū
oysters	*çippi, ippi*	shippi, ippi
parrot	*kiḷi*	ki*l*i
paw	*nagam*	nugŭm
peafowl	*mayil*	muyil
pig	*paṉṟi*	pundri
pigeon	*puṟā*	pūrrah
prawn	*iṟāl*	irrahl
quail	*kāḍāi*	kahd*ay*
rat	*eli*	(y)eli
salt fish	*uppu-mīṉ*	ūppū-meen
— — (dried)	*karuvāḍu*	kurūvahdū
salt-pan *or* pit	*upp'aḷam*	ūpp'u*l*ŭm
shark	*çuṟā-mīṉ*	shūrrah-meen
sheep	*āḍu*	ahdū
shrimp	*iṟavu*	(y)irruvū
silkworm	*paṭṭu-nūṭ-pūcci*	puttū-noo*t*-pooch-chi
snake	*pāmbu*	pahmbū
snipe	*uḷḷāṉ-kuruvi*	ū*ll*ahn-kūrūvi

English.	Tamil (romanized).	Pronunciation.
sparrow	*ūrkkuruvi*	oork-kūrūvi
spider	*çilandi*	shilun*thi*
squirrel	*aṉil*	u*n*il
stork	*nārāi, kokku*	nahr*ay*, kokkū
swallow	*tūkkaṇaṅ-kuruvi*	thookkū*n*ūng-kūrūvi
swan	*aṉṉa-p-paṭci*	unnūp-putchi
tail	*vāl*	vahl
teal	*çiṟagi, kiḷuvāi*	shirrūghi, ki*l*ūv*ay*
tiger	*puli*	pūli
trout	*āṯṯu-* (or *kuḷa'-*) *mīṉ*	ah*tt*ū- (*or* kū*la*'-) meen
turkey	*vāṉ-kōḻi*	vahn-koh-ryi
turtle (tortoise)	*āmāi*	ahm*ay*
vulture	*irājāḷi*	irahjah*l*i
whiting	*kiṟaṅgāṉ-mīṉ*	kiryūng-gahn-meen
wing	*çiṟagu*	shirrūgū
wolf	*ōnāy*	ohnahy
woodpecker	*taccaṉ-kuruvi*	thuch-chūn-kūrūvi
wood-pigeon	*kāṭṭup-puṟā*	kahttūp-pūrrah

5. Trees, Fruits, Flowers, Vegetables, &c.

(*Maraṅgaḷ, paṟaṅgaḷ, pūgaḷ, kīrāigaḷ, mudalāṉavāigaḷ.*)

(See Shopping, p. 69.)

English.	Tamil (romanized).	Pronunciation.
Apple (wood-)	*viḷām-paṟam* [*nuṇā*	vilahm-puryūm [inūnah
— (custard-)	*çīttāp-paṟam, aṇi-*	sheeth-thahp-puryūm, *un-*
— (jujube-)	*ilandāip-paṟam*	ilunth*ay*p-puryūm
— (rose-)	*jambu-nāvaṯ-paṟam*	jumbū nahvūt-puryūm
banana (fruit)	*vāṟāippaṟam*	vah-ry*ay*p-puryūm
bark	*paṭṭāi*	put*tay*
beans	*avarāi*	uvūr*ay*
bouquet	*pūñ-çeṇḍu*	poo*ng*-she*n*dū
branch	*kombu*	kombū
cabbage, cauli-	*kōvis-kīrāi*	gohvis-keer*ay*
chilli [flower	*milagāy*	mi*l*ūgahy
cinnamon	*karuvāp-paṭṭāi*	kurrūvahp-putt*ay*
cloves	*kirāmbu*	kirahmbū
cocoanut	*tēṅgāy*	thayng-gahy
cocoanut-palm	*teṉṉa-maram*	thennū-murūm
cucumber	*kakkari, veḷḷarikkāy*	kukkūri, ve*ll*ūrikkahy
ebony	*karuṅgāli*	kurūng-gahli
fern	*nīrvēmbu*	neervaymbū

English.	Tamil (romanized).	Pronunciation.
fig	*attip-paṛam*	uththip-puryŭm
fig-tree	*atti-maram*	uththi-murŭm
— (banian)	*āla-maram*	ahlŭ-murŭm
fir-tree	*tēvadāru*	*th*ayvŭ*th*ahrŭ
flower	*pū*	poo
garlic	*veḷḷäi-veṅgāyam*	ve*ll*ay-veng-gahyŭm
ginger	*iñji*	i*ng*ji
— (dried)	*çukku*	shŭkkŭ
grapes	*mundirigäip-paṛam*	mŭn*th*irig*ay*p-puryŭm
kernel	*koṭṭäi, paruppu*	kott*ay*, purŭppŭ
leaf	*iläi*	(y)il*ay*
lemon	*elumiccäi*	(y)elŭmich-ch*ay*
lily (water-)	*tāmaräi*	thahmŭr*ay*
lime	*elumiccaṅ-gāy*	(y)elŭmich-chŭng-gahy
mace	*çādipattiri*	jah*th*iputh-thiri
mango	*māṅgāy, mām-*	mahng-gahy, mahm-
melon	*kommaṭṭi* [*paṛam*	kommutti [puryŭm
mulberry	*muçukkaṭṭäiccedi*	mŭshŭkkutt*ay*ch-chedi
nut	*koṭṭäi*	kott*ay*
nutmeg	*çādikkāy*	jah*th*ikkahy
oak-tree	*karuvāli-maram*	kurŭvahli-murŭm
olive	*olīva-maram*	oleevŭ-murŭm
opium	*abiṉ*	ubin
orange	*nārattam-paṛam*	nahrŭth-thŭm-puryŭm
palmyra palm	*paṉäi*	pun*ay*
peas	*payaṟu*	puyŭrrŭ
pepper	*miḷagu*	mi*l*ŭgŭ
pineapple	*aṉṉāçip-paṛam*	unnahship-puryŭm
plantain	*vāṛäip-paṛam*	vahry*ay*p-puryŭm
plum	*tirāṭcap-paṛam*	thirahtchŭp-puryŭm
pomegranate	*mādaḷäi*	mah*th*ŭ*l*ay
poppy	*kaçakaçā*	kushŭkushah
potatoes	*uruḷäik-kiṛaṅgu*	ŭrŭ*l*ayk-kiryŭnggŭ
rape-seed	*eḷḷu*	(y)e*ll*ŭ
reed	*nāṇal*	nah*n*ŭl
root	*vēr, kiṛaṅgu*	vayr, kiryŭnggŭ
rose	*muṭcevvandi, rōçā*	mŭtchevvŭn*th*i, rohshah
saffron	*mañjaḷ*	mu*ng*jŭ*l*
sago	*javvariçi*	juvvurishi
tea-leaf	*tē-yiläi*	thay-yil*ay*

English	Tamil (romanized).	Pronunciation.
teak-tree	*tēkku*	thaykkū
tobacco	*pugäi-yiläi*	pūgay-yilay
tomato	*takkāḷi*	tukkahli
tree-trunk	*aḍi-maram*	udi-murūm
vine	*tirāṭcakkoḍi*	thirahtchūk-kodi
walnut	*kaḍukkāy*	kudūkkahy

6. Colours. (*Niraṅgaḷ.*)

English	Tamil (romanized).	Pronunciation.
Black	*karuppu*	kurrūppū
blue	*nīlam*	neelūm
brown	*ūdā-niram*	oothah-nirrūm
crimson	*karuñ-çivappu*	kurūng-shivūppū
dark	*kār-niram*	kahr-nirrūm
green	*paccäi, paçumäi*	puch-chay, pushūmay
grey	*veḷiriṇa-niram*	velirrinū-nirrūm
light (pale)	*maṅganiram*	munggū'nirrūm
orange	*çembīdam*	shembeethūm
pink	*ilañ-çivappu, pāṭa-[lam*	ilūng-shivuppū, pahtūlum
purple	*indira-nīlam* / *tūmira-varṇam*	inthirū-neelūm / thoomirū-vurnūm
red	*çivappu, çemmäi*	shivuppū, shemmay
violet	*nīla-çemmäi*	neelū-shemmay
white	*veṇmäi, veḷḷäi*	venmay, vellay
yellow	*mañjaḷ-niram*	mungjul-nirrūm

7. Times and Seasons. (*Kāla-vagäi.*)

(For Conversations see page 55.)

English	Tamil (romanized).	Pronunciation.
Afternoon	*pinnēram, piṯpagal*	pinnayrūm, pilpugūl
birthday	*piranda-nāḷ*	pirrunthū-nahl
Christmas	*Kiristu-piranda-[pandigäi*	kirristhū-pirrunthū-pun-[digay
date	*tēdi*	thaythi
dawn	*viḍiyaṯ-kālam*	vidiyūt-kahlūm
day	*nāḷ, tinam*	nahl, thinūm
day-time	*pagal*	pugūl
day, to-	*inru, inräikku*	indrū, indraykkū
days of the week	*kiramäigaḷ*	kiryūmaygūl
Sunday	*ñāyiṯṯuk-kiramäi*	nyahyittūk-kiryūmay
Monday	*tiṅgaṯ-kiramäi*	thinggūt-kiryūmay
Tuesday	*çevvāyk-kiramäi*	shevvahyk-kiryūmay
Wednesday	*pudan-kiramäi*	pūthūn-kiryūmay

English.	Tamil (romanized).	Pronunciation.
Thursday	*viyāṛak-kiṛamäi*	viyahryŭk-kiryŭm*ay*
Friday	*veḻḻik-kiṛamäi*	ve*ll*ik-kiryŭm*ay*
Saturday	*çaṉik-kiṛamäi*	shunik-kiryŭm*ay*
Easter	*Kiṟistu uyirtt'eṛunda tirunāḻ*	kirristhū ūyirthth'eryŭn *th*ū thirū-nah*l*
evening	*çāyaṅ-kālam*	shahyŭng-kahlŭm
fortnight	*iraṇḍu-kiṛamäi*	iru*n*dū-kiryŭm*ay*
Good-Friday	*peru-veḻḻik-kiṛamäi*	perū-ve*ll*ik-kiryŭm*ay*
holiday	*vāvu*	vahvū
hour	*ōräi, maṇi-nēram*	ohr*ay*, mu*n*i-nayrŭm
—, half-an-	*aräi-maṇi-nēram*	ur*ay*-mu*n*i-nayrŭm
—, Tamil (24 [minutes)	*nāṛigäi*	nah-ryig*ay*
mid day	*mattiyāṉam*	muth-thiyahnŭm
midnight	*nadurāttiri*	nudū-rahth-thiri
Midsummer	*naḍuk-kōḍäi*	nudūk-kohd*ay*
minute	*viṉāḍi, nimiçam*	vinahdi, nimishŭm
month	*mādam, māçam*	mah*th*ŭm, mahshŭm
month by month	*māça-māçam*	mahsha-mahshŭm
months (the)	*mādaṅgaḻ*	mah*th*ŭng-gŭ*l*
April-May	*çittiräi*	shith-thir*ay*
May-June	*vaigāçi*	v*i*gahshi
June-July	*āṉi*	ahni
July-August	*āḍi*	ahdi
August-Sept.	*āvaṇi*	ahvŭ*n*i
September-Oct.	*puraṭṭāçi*	pūruttahshi
October-Nov.	*aippaçi*	*i*ppushi
November-Dec.	*kārttigäi*	kahrth-thig*ay*
December-Jan.	*mārgaṛi*	mahr-gŭryi
January-Feb.	*tai*	th*i*
February-March	*māçi*	mahshi
March-April	*paṅguṉi*	punggŭni
morning	*kālamē, kāläi*	kahlŭmay, kahl*ay*
this morning	*iṉṟu-kālamē*	indrū-kahlŭmay
to-morrow	*nāḻäi, nāḻäikku*	nah*lay*, nah*lay*kkū
night	*irā, irāttiri*	irah, irahth-thiri
noon	*nadup-pagal*	nudūp-pugŭl
seasons:	*kālaṅgaḻ*	kahlŭnggŭ*l*
Spring	*vaçanta-kālam*	vushŭnthŭ-kahlŭm
Summer	*kōḍäik-kālam*	kohd*ay*k-kahlŭm
Autumn	*kaṉi-kālam*	kuni-kahlŭm

English.	Tamil (romanized).	Pronunciation.
Winter	*çītaḷa-kālam*	sheetŭ*l*ŭ-kahlŭm
rainy season	*māri-kālam*	mahri-kahlŭm
second	*nimiçam*	nimishŭm
sunrise	*udayam*	ūt*h*ŭyŭm
sunset	*astamaṉam*	usthŭmŭnŭm
week	*vāram, kiṛamäi*	vahrŭm, kiryŭm*ay*
year	*varusham, āṇḍu*	vurūshŭm, ah*n*dū
yesterday	*nēṯṯu*	nay*tt*ū

8. Town and Country. (*Nāṭṭu-vagäi.*)

(For Conversations see page 57.)

Bridge	*pālam*	pahlŭm
cathedral	*piradāṉa dēvālayam*	pirūdahnū *th*ayvahlŭyŭm
church	*kōvil, dēvālayam*	kohvil, *th*ayvahlŭyŭm
country	*nāḍu, dēçam*	nahdū, *th*ayshŭm
ditch	*agaṛ, paḷḷam*	ugŭry, pu*ll*ŭm
farm	*kambattam, kāṇi*	kumbuth-thŭm, kah*ni*
farmer	*vēḷāṇmäikkāraṉ,*	vay*l*ah*n*-m*ay*kkahrŭn,
	payir-çeygiṟavaṉ	puyir-sheyghirŭvŭn
fence	*vēli*	vayli
field	*vayal, veḷi*	vuyŭl, ve*l*i
foot-path	*aḍippāḍu, çiṟu-pā-*	udippahdū, shirū-pah-
forest	*kāḍu, vaṉam* [*däi*	kahdū, vunŭm [*thay*
gate	*vāçal*	vahshŭl
grass	*pul*	pūl
hut	*kuḍiçäi*	kudish*ay*
inn	*çattiram*	shuth-thirŭm
jungle	*kāḍu*	kahdū
log	*kaṭṭäi*	kutt*ay*
market	*kaḍäi*	kud*ay*
meadow	*puṯṯaräi, paçumpuṉ-*	pū*tt*ŭr*ay*, pushŭm-pŭn-
mile	*mayil* [*ṉilam*	muyil [nilŭm
mill	*ēndiram, tirigäi*	ayn*th*irŭm, thirig*ay*
monument	*ñābagakkuṟippu*	nyahbŭgŭkkŭrrippū
palace	*araṉmaṉäi, māḷigäi*	urŭ*n*mun*ay*, mah*l*ig*ay*
road	*vaṛi*	vu-ryi
school	*paḷḷikkūḍam*	pu*ll*ikkoodŭm
shepherd	*mēyppaṉ, iḍäiyaṉ*	mayp-pŭn, id*ay*yŭn
shop	*kaḍäi, çāppu*	kud*ay*, shahppū
sign-post	*vaṛi-kāṭṭi-tū-*	vuryi-kahtti-thoon

English.	Tamil (romanized).	Pronunciation.
square	*çatukkam*	shuthŭkkŭm
straw	*vaikkōl*	vikkohl
street	*teru, vīdi*	therŭ, vee*thi*
temple	*kōvil, dēvastānam*	kohvil, *th*ayvŭsthahnŭm
town	*nagaram, paṭṭaṇam*	nugŭrŭm, puttŭ*n*ŭm
town-hall	*nagara-māḷigäi*	nugŭrŭ-mah*ligay*
university	*sarva-kalā-çaṅgam*	survŭ-kulah-sung-gŭm
village	*ūr, girāmam*	oor, ghirahmŭm

9. Mankind: Relations. (*Nara-vagäi: uṟavu-muṟäi.*)

Aunt; mother-in-	*māmi, attäi*	mahmi, uth-th*ay*
brother (elder) [law	*aṇṇan, tamäiyan*	u*n*nŭn, thum*ayy*ŭn
— (younger)	*tambi* [*nan*	thumbi [nŭn
— -in-law; cousin	*maittunan, macci-*	m*i*th-thŭnŭn, much-chi-
cousin (*f.*); sister-in-law	*maittuni, maccinicci*	m*i*th-thŭni, much-chi-nich-chi
daughter	*magaḷ, kumāratti*	mugŭ*l*, kŭmahrŭth-thi
daughter-in-law	*marumagaḷ*	murŭmugŭ*l*
father	*tagappan, tandäi*	thugŭppŭn, thun*thay*
father-in-law	*māman*	mahmŭn
father's father	*tātā, pāṭṭan*	thah-thah, paht-tŭn
— elder brother	*periya tagappan*	periyŭ thugŭppŭn
— younger do.	*çiṟiya tagappan*	shirriyŭ thugŭppŭn
— mother	*pāṭṭi*	pahtti
— sister	*attäi*	uth-th*ay*
— sister's husband	*ammān*	ummahn
grand-son; -daugh-	*pēran; pērtti*	payrŭn; payrth-thi
husband [ter	*puruçan*	pŭrŭshŭn
husband's sister	*nātti*	nahth-thi
man	*maṉidan, āḷ*	muni*th*ŭn, ah*l*
mother	*tāy, ammā*	thahy, ummah
mother's father	*pāṭṭan*	pahttŭn
— mother	*ammāyi*	ummahyi
sister (elder)	*akkāḷ*	ukkah*l*
— (younger)	*taṅgäi*	thung-ga*y*
son	*magan, puttiran*	mugŭn, pŭth-thirŭn
son-in-law	*marumagan*	murŭmugŭn
stepmother	*maṟu-tāy*	murrŭ-thahy
uncle (mother's	*māman*	mahmŭn
widow [brother)	*kaim-peṇ, vidavai*	kim-pe*n*, vi*th*ŭvay

English.	Tamil (romanized).	Pronunciation.
widower	*dāram-irandavan*	*th*ahrūm-iryun*th*ŭvŭn
wife	*manäivi, pençādi*	mun*ay*vi, pe*n*shah*thi*
— (elder)	*mūtta-dāram*	mooth-thŭ-*th*ahrŭm
— (younger)	*iläiya-dāram*	il*ay*yŭ-*th*ahrŭm
wife's sister	*korundi*	koryŭn*thi*
woman	*stiri, pen*	sthiri, pe*n*

10. The Human Body. (*Çarīrāvayavangaļ.*)

Ankle	*kaṇukkāl*	ku*n*ukkahl
arm	*buyam, karam*	būyŭm, kurŭm
arm-pit	*kakkam, akkuļ*	kukkŭm, ukku*l*
back	*mudugu*	mū*th*ŭgū
beard	*tāḍi, mīçäi*	thahdi, meeshay
blood	*irattam, udiram*	iruththŭm, ū*th*irŭm
body	*çarīram, uḍambu*	shureerŭm, ūdŭmbū
bones	*elumbu*	elŭmbū
bowels	*kuḍal*	kūdŭl
brain	*mūḷäi, buddi*	moo*lay*, bŭddi
breast, chest	*mārbu, neñju*	mahrbū, ne*ng*jŭ
cheek	*kannam*	kunnŭm
chin	*mōvāykkaṭṭäi*	mohvahykkutt*ay*
complexion	*çarīra-varṇam*	shureerŭ-vu*r*nŭm
ears (external)	*kādu, çevi*	kah*th*ū, shevi
elbow	*muraṅ-kai*	mūryŭng-*ki*
eye; eyeball	*kaṇ; kaṇ-viḷi*	ku*n*; ku*n*-viryi
eyebrow	*neṯṯippuruvam*	ne*tt*ippūrŭvŭm
eyelid	*kaṇ-maḍal*	ku*n*-mudŭl
face	*mugam*	mŭgum
fingers	*kai-viral, aṅguli*	*ki*-virŭl, ung-gūli
foot	*aḍi, pādam*	udi, pahthŭm
forehead	*neṯṯi, nudal*	ne*tt*i, nū*th*ŭl
groin	*aräippūṭṭu*	ur*ay*ppoottŭ
hair	*mayir, urōmam*	muyir, ŭrohmŭm
hand	*kai*	*ki*
head	*taläi, çiraçu*	thul*ay*, shirŭshū
heart	*irudayam*	irū*th*ŭyŭm
heel	*kudikkāl*	kū*th*ikkahl
hip	*iḍuppu*	idūppū
jaw	*tāḍäi, alagu*	thahd*ay*, ulŭgū
kidneys	*māṅgāyīral, nīrīral*	mahng-gahy-eerŭl, neer- [eerŭl

English.	Tamil (romanized).	Pronunciation.
knee	*muṛaṅ-kāl*	mūryŭng-kahl
leg	*kāl*	kahl
lip	*uḍaḍu*	ŭthŭdū
liver	*īral, kallīral*	eerŭl, kulleerŭl
lung	*veḷḷīral, çuvāçāça-*	velleerŭl, shuvahshah-
moustache	*mīçäi [yam*	meeshay [shŭyŭm
mouth	*vāy*	vahy
nails	*nagam*	nugŭm
neck	*kaṛuttu*	kuryuth-thū
nose	*mūkku, nāçi*	mookkū, nahshi
ribs	*vilā-v-elumbu*	vilah-v-elūmbū
shoulders	*tōḷ, buyam*	thohl, būyŭm
side	*vilā*	vilah
skin	*tōl*	tohl
skull	*taläiyōḍu, manḍäi*	thulayyohdū, munday
spine	*mudug'elumbu*	mūthŭg'elūmbū
stomach	*vayiṟu, iräikkuḍal*	vuyirū, iraykkūdŭl
temples	*kaṉṉappoṟi*	kunnŭpporri
throat	*tonḍäi*	thonday
thumb	*peruviral*	perūvirŭl
toe	*kāl-viral*	kahl-virŭl
tongue	*nā, nākku*	nah, nahkkū
tooth	*pal*	pul
wrist	*maṇikkaṭṭu*	munikkuttū

11. Health. (*Çostattäi-k-kuṟittu.*)

(For Conversations see page 54.)

English.	Tamil (romanized).	Pronunciation.
Accident	*iḍäiyūṟu*	idayyoorrū
bandage	*kavaṇam, kāyakkaṭ-*	kuvŭnŭm, kahyŭkkuttū
bile	*pittam [ṭu*	pith-thŭm
bite	*kaḍi*	kudi
—, snake-	*pāmbu-kaḍi*	pahmbū-kudi
blindness	*kuruḍu*	kūrūdū
blister	*koppuḷam*	koppūlum
bruise	*naçivu [kāyam*	nushivū [yŭm
burn	*çūḍu, çūḍ'unda-*	shoodū, shood'ŭndŭ-kah-
chemist's shop	*marunduccālāi*	murŭnthŭch-chahlay
chill	*kuḷir*	kūlir
cholera	*vāndi-pēdi*	vahnthi-pāythi
contagion	*toṭṭu-viyādi*	thot-tū-viyahthi

English.	Tamil (romanized).	Pronunciation.
corns	*āṇi, kāyppū*	ah*n*i, kahyppū
cough	*irumal*	irūmŭl
cramp	*vali, īrppu*	vuli, eerppū
cure	*parikāram*	purikahrŭm
deaf	*çeviḍu*	shevidū
dentist	*danta-vaittiyan̲*	*th*unthŭ-v*i*ththiyŭn
diarrhœa	*vayit̲t̲uppōkku*	v*itt*ūppohkkū [yŭm
diet	*çāppāḍu, pattiyam*	shahppahdū, puth-thi-
disease, illness	*viyādi, nōy*	viyah*th*i, nohy
doctor	*vaittiyan̲*	v*i*ththiyŭn
draught	*marunduk-kuḍippu*	murŭnthŭk-kūdippū
dumb	*ūmäi, mūgäi* [*ram*	oom*ay*, moog*ay* [shahrŭm
dysentery	*iratta-pēdi, atiçā-*	iruth-thŭ-pay*th*i, uthi-
exercise	*paṛakkam, payil̲ci*	puryŭkkŭm, puyi*t*chi
to faint	*mūrcci*	moorch-chi
fatigue	*iḷaippu*	i*lay*ppū
fever	*kāyccal, juram*	kahych-chŭl, jūrŭm
— and ague	*naḷir-juram*	nu*l*ir-jūrŭm
—, enteric	*viça-juram*	vishŭ-jūrŭm
—, intermittent	*mur̲äikkāyccal*	mūrr*ay*kkahych-chŭl
fracture	*uḍäivu*	ud*ay*vū [rohgŭm
gout	*çūläi-nōy, vāta-rō-*	shool*ay*-nohy, vahthŭ-
headache	*taläi-nōvu* [*gam*	thul*ay*-nohvū
ill, sick	*çugam-illāda, çuga-*	shūgŭm-illah*th*ŭ, shūgŭ-
indigestion	*açīraṇam* [*vīn̲a*	usheerŭ*n*ŭm [veenŭ
inflammation	*erivu*	erivū
lame	*noṇḍi*	no*n*di
medicine	*marundu, auçadam*	murŭn*th*ū, owshŭ*th*ŭm
nurse	*tādi, kait-tāy, çevi-*	thah*th*i, k*i*th-thahy, shevi-
ointment	*tailam* [*littāy*	th*i*lŭm [lith-thahy
pain	*nōvu, uḷäivu, vali*	nohvū, ūl*ay*vū, vuli
paralysis	*timir*	thimir
pill	*māttiräi*	mahth-thir*ay*
poison	*nañju, viçam* [*nāgam*	nu*n*gjū, vishŭm [nahgŭm
poultice	*pukkäi, pat̲t̲u, uba-*	pūkk*ay*, pu*tt*ū, ūbŭ-
prescription	*vāgaḍamur̲äi*	vahgūdŭmūrr*ay*
quinine	*kinin-marundu*	kinin-murŭn*th*ū
remedy	*parikāram*	purikahrŭm
rest	*iḷäippāt̲t̲i, oyvu*	i*lay*ppah*tt*i, oyvū
scald	*venda-puṇ*	ven*th*ŭ-pū*n*

English.	Tamil (romanized).	Pronunciation.
scratch	*kīṟu, piṟāṇḍu*	keerrū, pirrah*n*dū
sore	*puṇ*	pū*n*
sprain	*çuḷukku, uḷukku*	shū*l*ūkkū, ū*l*ūkkū
sting	*koḍukku*	kodūkkū
surgeon	*çattira-vaittiyaṉ*	shuth-thirū-viththiyūn
tonic	*balavirttiyauçadam*	bulū-virththi-yowshū-[*th*ūm
wound	*kāyam, puṇ*	kahyūm, pū*n*

12. Food and Drink. (*Aṉṉapāṉam.*)

See also pages 15 to 19. For Conversations see pages 53—54.)

English.	Tamil (romanized).	Pronunciation.
Bacon	*paṉṟi-yiṟäicci-vaṭ-[ṭal*	pundriyirr*ay*chchi-vu*tt*ūl
beef	*māṭṭiṟäicci*	mahttirr*ay*ch-chi
bottle	*çittäi, puṭṭi, çīçā*	shith-th*ay*, būtti, shee-[shah
bread	*uroṭṭi, appam*	ūrotti, uppūm
breakfast	*kāläiccāppāḍu*	kahl*ay*ch-chahppahdū
butter	*veṇṇey*	ve*n*ney
cake	*paṇiyāram*	pu*n*iyahrūm
cheese	*pālāḍäikkaṭṭi*	pahlahd*ay*kkutti
chocolate	*çokolēṭ*	shokolayt
claret	*kilaraṭ*	kilūrūt
coffee	*kāppi*	kahppi
cream	*āḍäi, pālēḍu*	ahd*ay*, pahlaydū
curry	*kaṟi*	kurri
dinner	*tīṉi*	theeni
eggs	*muṭṭäi*	mūtt*ay*
fat	*koṛuppu, ney*	koryūppū, ney
fish	*mīṉ*	meen
flour	*mā*	mah
honey	*tēṉ, madu*	thayn, mu*th*ū
ice	*uṟainda nīr* [*jām*	ūrr*ay*n*th*ū neer
jam	*iṉippukkuṟambu,*	inippūkkūryūmbū, jahm
kidney	*māṅgāyīral*	mahng-gahy-eerūl [chi
lamb	*çemmaṟiyāṭṭiṟäicci*	shemmūrriyahtt'irr*ay*ch-
lemonade	*elumiccampaṛa-raçapāṉa*	elūmichchūm-puryū-rushūpahnū
luncheon	*ttippiṉ, çiṭṭuṇā*	tiffin, shi*tt*ū*n*ah
meat	*iṟäicci* [*yaṭkaṟi*	irr*ay*ch-chi [kurri
—, boiled	*aviyaliṟäicci, avi-*	uviyūlirraychchi, uviyū*t*-
—, roast	*çuṭṭaviṟäicci*	shūttūvirr*ay*ch-chi
milk	*pāl*	pahl

English.	Tamil (romanized).	Pronunciation.
mustard	*kaḍugu*	kudūgū
mutton	*āṭṭiṟāicci*	ahttirraych-chi
oil	*eṇṇey, ney*	enney, ney
onion	*veṅgāyam*	veng-gahyŭm
pepper	*miḷagu*	milūgū
pork	*paṉṟi-yiṟāicci*	pundri-yirraych-chi
port wine	*pōrt vain*	pohrt-vin
pudding	*piṭṭu*	pittū
rice, raw husked	*ariçi*	urishi
—, boiled	*çōṟu*	shohrru
— cakes	*āppam*	ahppŭm
salad	*çallādu-kkīrāi*	shullahthū-kkeeray
salt	*uppu*	ūppū
sherry	*çeṟi vain*	sherri vin
soda-water	*uvar-nīr*	ūvŭr-neer
soup	*kuṟambu, āṇam*	kūryŭmbū, ahnŭm
sugar	*çīṉi, çarkkarāi*	sheeni, shurkkūray
supper	*irābbōjaṉam*	irahbbohjūnŭm
tea (beverage)	*tē-nīr*	thay-neer
tobacco	*pugāiyilāi*	pūgay-yilay
under-done	*kuṟāiyacceyda, kuṟāiyaccuṭṭa*	kūrrayyŭch-cheythŭ, kūrrayyŭch-chūttū
veal	*kaṉṟ'iṟāicci*	kundr'irraych-chi
vegetable	*marakkaṟi, pūḍu*	murūkkurri, poodū
vinegar	*kāḍi*	kahdi
water	*nīr*	neer
—, cold	*taṇṇīr*	thunneer
—, hot	*veṇṇīr*	venneer
well-done	*naṉṟāycceyda, naṉṟāyccuṭṭa*	nundrahych-cheythŭ, nundrahych-chūttū
wine	*tirāṭçā-raçapāṉam*	thirahtshah-rushūpah-nŭm

13. Cooking and Eating Utensils. (*Çaṭṭi-pāṉāigaḷ.*)

(For Shopping see page 59.)

English.	Tamil (romanized).	Pronunciation.
Basin	*kalaçam*	kulūshŭm
bowl	*kiṇṇam, pāttiram*	kinnŭm, pahth-thirum
coffee-pot	*kōppip-pōccu*	kohppi-p-pohch-chū
corkscrew	*kucciḍukki*	kuchch'idūkki
cruet-stand	*kuppittaṭṭu*	kūppith-thuttū
cup	*kōppāi, kiṇṇam*	kohppay, kinnŭm

English.	Tamil (romanized).	Pronunciation.
dish	*taṭṭu, tālam, vaṭṭil*	thuttū, thahlŭm, vuttil
fork	*muḷḷu*	mūllū
frying-pan	*porikkuñçaṭṭi*	porikkūngshutti
glass (tumbler)	*paḷiṅgukkiṇṇam,*	puling-gūkkinnŭm,
grill	*girīl [tambaḷar*	gireel [thumbŭlŭr
kettle	*kēṭṭal, kopparäi*	kayttŭl, koppŭray
knife	*katti*	kuththi
ladle	*agappäi, karaṇḍi*	uguppay, kurŭndi
lid	*mūḍi*	moodi
matches	*tīkkuccu, tiri*	theekkŭch-chū, thiri
oven	*aḍuppu, çuḍuçūḷäi*	udūppū, shūdūshoolay
pan	*çaṭṭi*	shutti
plate	*pīṅgāṉ, tagaḍu*	peeng-gahn, thugŭdū
— of leaves	*kallāi [ṉäi*	kullay [pahnay
saucepan, pot	*ānaccaṭṭi, çāçuppā-*	ahnŭch-chutti,shahshūp-
saucer	*tālam, pīris, taṭṭu*	thahlŭm, peeris, thuttū
serviette	*kaikkuṭṭäi, kaittuvā-*	kikkūttay, kiththūvahlay
spoon	*karaṇḍi [läi*	kurŭndi
—, dessert-	*arakkaraṇḍi*	urŭkkurŭndi
—, table-	*ālakkaraṇḍi*	ahlukkurŭndi
—, tea-	*uccik-karaṇḍi*	ūchchik-kurŭndi
table-cloth	*mēçäittuppaṭṭi*	mayshayththūpputti
tea-pot	*tēkkeṇḍi, tēppōccu*	thaykkendi, thayppohch-
tray	*taṭṭu*	thuttū [chū
wineglass	*vayiṉ gilās*	vin ghilahs

14. Dress and Dressing. (*Uḍuppu-vagäi.*)

(See also Vocabulary 15, and Shopping, p. 59.)

English.	Tamil (romanized).	Pronunciation.
Boots	*neḍuñ çappāttu, neḍuñjōḍu*	nedungshuppahth-thū, nedūngjohdū
bracelet	*kaṅgaṇam, kāppu*	kung-gŭnŭm, kahppū
braces	*kaccu*	kuch-chū
brush	*kuccu, tūrigäi*	kūch-chū, thoorigay
buttons	*kumiṛ, teṟi*	kŭmiry, therri
button-hook	*teṟipūṭṭu*	therripoottū
calico	*pañjunūṭpuḍaväi*	pungjū-noot-pūdŭvay
cap (cloth)	*kullā, çiṟu toppi*	kūllah, shirrū thoppi
cloak, cape	*pōrväi, kuppāyam*	pohrvay, kūppahyŭm
cloth	*puḍaväi*	pūdŭvay
clothes-brush	*uḍupputtuḍäippam*	ūdūppūth-thūdayppŭm

English.	Tamil (romanized).	Pronunciation.
coat	*neḍuñ-çaṭṭäi*	nedu*ng*-shutt*ay*
comb	*çīppu*	sheeppū
cotton	*pañju-nūl*	pu*ng*jū-nool
dress (clothing)	*uḍuppu, vastiram*	ūdūppū, vustirūm
flannel	*kambaḷippuḍavăi*	kumbū*l*ippūdūv*ay*
gloves	*kai-yuṟäi*	k*i*-yūrr*ay*
hair-pin	*koṇḍäik-kuccu*	ko*n*d*ay*k-kūch-chū
hat	*toppi*	thoppi
jewellery	*paṇiḍi, ābaraṇam*	pu*n*i*th*i, ahbūrū*n*ūm
lace	*piṉṉal, çarigäi*	pinnūl, shurig*ay*
linen	*çaṇaṉūṯpuḍavăi*	shu*n*ūnoo*t*pūdūv*ay*
mirror	*kaṇṇāḍi*	ku*nn*ahdi
muslin	*kavaṇi, çallā*	kuvū*n*i, shullah
necklace	*kōväi*	kohv*ay*
necktie	*kaṟuttukkuṭṭäi*	kuryūththūk-kūtt*ay*
needle	*ūçi*	ooshi
overcoat	*mēṯçaṭṭäi*	may*t*shutt*ay*
parasol	*çiṟu-kuḍäi*	shirrū-kūd*ay*
pins	*kuṇḍūçi*	kū*n*dooshi
pocket	*çaṭṭäiccākku*	shutt*ay*ch-chahkkū
purse	*paṇappai*	pu*n*ūpp*i*
razor	*çavarak-katti*	shuvūrūk-kuththi
ring (for finger)	*mōdiram*	moh*th*irūm
scissors	*kattari*	kuth-thūri
shoe-lace	*çeruppiṉ vār*	sherūppin vahr
silk	*paṭṭu*	puttū
skirt	*pāvāḍäi*	pahvahd*ay*
slippers	*çeruppu, jōḍu*	sherūppū, johdū
soap	*çavukkāram*	shuvūkkahrūm
thread	*nūl*	nool
tooth-brush	*paṯkūrccu*	pu*t*koorch-chū
trousers	*kāṯcaṭṭäi*	kah*t*chutt*ay*
umbrella	*kuḍäi*	kūd*ay*
veil	*mukkāḍu*	mūkkahdū
walking-stick	*paṯṯukkōl*	pu*t*tūkkohl
watch	*kaḍiyāram*	gudi*y*ahrūm
waterproof coat	*maṟäiccaṭṭäi*	mury*ay*ch-chutt*ay*
wool	*kambaḷi*	kumbū*l*i

15. Washing List. (*Karuvum pudaväigal.*)

(Add *gal* to form the plural.)

English.	Tamil (romanized).	Pronunciation.
Apron	*mun-tängi*	mūn-thahng-ghi
bathing-dress	*kuli-çiläi*	kūli-sheelay
bed-clothes	*kattil-tuppatti*	kuttil-thūpputti
blanket	*kambalam*	kumbŭlŭm
bodice	*ravikkäi, çōli*	ruvikkay, shohli
cap	*çiru toppi, kullā*	shirrū thoppi, kūllah
chemise	*ullangi*	ūllungghi
collar	*karuttup-pattäi*	kuryūth-thūp-puttay
combinations	*magalīr utçattäi*	mugŭleer ūtshuttay
coverlet	*tuppatti, pōrppu*	thūpputti, pohrppū
cuff	*kaipattäi*	kiputtay
drawers (a pair)	*jalladam,* *utkātcattäi*	jullŭdŭm, ūtkahtchuttay
dress (gown)	*angi*	ungghi
flannel waistcoat	*kambali-mārbuccattäi*	kumbŭli-mahrbūchchuttay
handkerchief	*kaikkuttäi*	kikkūttay
jacket	*araiccattäi*	uraych-chuttay
napkin	*kaittuvāläi*	kittūvahlay
necktie	*karuttukkuttäi*	kuryūththuk-kūttay
night-dress	*irā-udäi*	irah-ūday
night-shirt	*irāk-kamiçu*	irahk-kumishū
pants (drawers), a pair	*utkātcattäi*	ūtkaht-chuttay
petticoat	*utpāvādäi*	ūtpahvahday
pillow-case	*taläiyanäi-y-uräi*	thulayyunay-yūrray
pinafore	*mun-tängi*	mūn-thahng-ghi
pyjamas	*pajāmā*	pujahmah
serviette	*kaikkuttäi*	kikkūttay
sheet	*tuppatti*	thūpputti
shirt	*kamiçu*	kumishū
socks (a pair)	*mējōdu, kāluräi*	mayjohdū, kahlūrray
stays „	*kaccu*	kuchchū
stockings „	*periya mējōdu*	periyŭ mayjohdū
table-cloth	*mēçäittuppatti*	mayshayth-thūpputti
towel	*tuvāläi*	thūvahlay
trousers (a pair)	*kātcattäi*	kahtchuttay
under-vest	*unmārbuccattäi*	ūnmahrbuch-chuttay
vest	*mārbuccattäi*	mahrbūch-chuttay

16. House and Furniture. (*Vīḍum adaṉ çāmāṉgaḷum.*)

(See also Vocabulary 13, page 27, and Shopping, page 59.)

English.	Tamil (romanized).	Pronunciation.
Ante-room	*naḍäiyaṟäi, ediraṟäi*	nud*ay*-yurr*ay*, et*h*ir-urr*ay*
arm-chair	*kaiyuḷḷa nāṯkāli*	k*i*yūllŭ nah*t*kahli
basket	*kūḍäi, peṭṭi*	kood*ay*, petti
bed	*paḍukkäi, kaṭṭil*	pudūkk*ay*, kuttil
bedroom	*paḍukkäi-y-aṟäi*	pudūkk*ay*-yurr*ay*
blind (window)	*jaṉṉal mūḍuñ tiräi*	junnŭl moodum thir*ay*
book-case	*pustagak-kūḍu*	pūsthŭgŭk-koodū
box	*peṭṭagam, peṭṭi*	pettŭgŭm, petti
broom	*tuḍaippam*	thūd*ay*ppŭm
candle	*merugu-tiri*	meryūgū-thiri
candlestick	*viḷakkuttaṇḍu*	vi*l*ukkūth-thu*n*dū
carpet	*çamukkāḷam*	shumūkkah*l*ŭm
chair	*nāṯkāli* [*māṉgaḷ*	nah*t*kahli [mahngŭ*l*
chamber utensils	*paḍukkäiyaṟäi çā-*	pudūkk*ay*yurr*ay* shah-
chest of drawers	*lāccippeṭṭi* [*kūḍu*	lahchchip-petti [koodū
chimney	*pugäi-vāyil, pugäik-*	pūg*ay*vahyil, pūg*ay*k-
closet (w.c.)	*uḷḷaṟäi, çiṯṯaṟäi*	ūllurr*ay*, shi*tt*urr*ay*
clock	*kaḍiyāram, oralōçi*	gudiyahrŭm, orŭlohshi
couch	*çārmaṉäi-k-kaṭṭil*	shahrmŭ*n*ay-k-kuttil
cupboard	*bōjaṉapāttirapīḍam*	bohjūnŭ-pahththirūpee-
curtain	*tiräi*	thir*ay* [dŭm
— (window)	*jaṉṉal tiräi-c-cīläi*	junnŭl thir*ay*-ch-cheel*ay*
cushion	*mettäi*	meth-th*ay*
dining-room	*çāppāṭṭaṟäi, bōjaṉa-*	shahppahtturr*ay*, bohjŭ-
door	*kadavu* [*çāläi*	kut*h*ŭvū [nŭ-shahl*ay*
door-bell (street-)	*terukkadavu-maṇi*	therūk-kut*h*ŭvū-mu*n*i
drawing-room	*virundaṟäi*	virūn*th*urr*ay*
easy chair	*çāymāṉa nāṯkāli*	shahymahnŭ nah*t*kahli
electric light	*miṉçāra veḷiccam*	minshahrū ve*l*ich-chŭm
fender	*tīttāṅgi*	theeth-thahng-ghi
fire	*neruppu, tī*	nerūppū, thee
fireplace	*aḍuppu*	udūppū
floor	*talam*	thu*l*ŭm
garden	*tōṭṭam, kolläi*	thohttŭm, koll*ay*
gas	*vāyuveḷiccam*	vahyū-ve*l*ich-chŭm
grate	*neruppuk-kirādi*	nerūppūk-kirah*thi*
hall (entrance)	*vāçal-çāläi*	vahshŭl shahl*ay*

English.	Tamil (romanized).	Pronunciation.
key	*çāvi*	shahvi
kitchen	*kuçiṉi*	kūshini
— dresser	*kuçiṉi-mēçäi*	kūshini-mayshay
lamp	*vilakku, tībam*	vilukkū, theebam [idum
larder	*iṟäicciyäi vaikkum*	irraych-chiyay vikkūm
library	*puttagaçālüi [iḍam*	pūth-thūgū-shahlay
lock	*pūṭṭu*	poottū
looking-glass	*niläikkaṇṇādi*	nilaykkunnahdi
piano	*kiṉṉāraṅ-kūḍu*	kinnahrūng-koodū
picture	*çittiram, paḍam*	shiththirum, pudūm
pillow	*taläiyaṇäi*	thulayyunay
poker	*tūṇḍu-kōl*	thoondū-kohl
roof	*kūräi*	kooray
room	*aṟäi*	urray
shelf	*taṭṭu*	thuttū
sideboard	*çuvarp-palagäi*	shūvūrp-pulūgay
staircase	*paḍikkaṭṭu*	pudikkuttū
stairs	*paḍigaḷ*	pudigūl
table	*mēçäi*	mayshay
table-cover	*mēçäittuppaṭṭi*	mayshayth-thūpputti
tiles	*ōḍu*	ohdū
tongs	*kuṟaḍu, iḍukki*	kūrrūdū, idūkki
vase	*pāttiram*	pahth-thirūm
verandah	*virāndā, tiṇṇäi*	virahnthah, thinnay
wall	*çuvar*	shūvūr
window	*jaṉṉal*	junnūl

17. Professions and Trades. (*Toṟilgaḷ.*)

(For Shopping see p. 59.)

English.	Tamil (romanized).	Pronunciation.
Architect	*çiṟpāçāri*	shitpah-shahri
artisan	*kammāḷaṉ, çiṟpaṉ*	kummahlūn, shitpūn
baker	*roṭṭikkāraṉ*	rottikkahrūn
banker	*çāvagāri*	shahvagahri
barber	*ambaṭṭaṉ, nāvidaṉ*	umbūttūn, nahvithūn
blacksmith	*kollaṉ*	kollūn
brazier	*kaṉṉāṉ*	kunnahn
bookseller	*pustaga-viyābāri*	pūstūgū-viyahbahri
butcher	*iṟäiccikkāraṉ*	irraych-chikkahrūn
carpenter	*taccaṉ [viyābāri*	thuch-chūn [yahbahri
chemist (druggist)	*marunduccarakku-*	murūndūchchurukkū-vi-

English.	Tamil (romanized).	Pronunciation.
clergyman	*pādiriyār*	pah*th*iriyahr
confectioner	*miṭṭāyikkāraṉ*	mittahyikkahrŭn
consul	*piratikāvalaṉ*	pirŭthikahvŭlŭn
cook	*çamäiyaṟkāraṉ*	shum*ayy*ŭ*t*kahrŭn
cycle-maker	*çakkara-çeygiṟavaṉ*	shukkŭrŭ-sheyghirrŭvŭn
dentist	*danta-vaittiyaṉ*	dunthŭ-*v*ith-thiyŭn
doctor	*vaittiyaṉ, parigāri*	vith-thiyŭn, purigahri
engineer	*çiṟpavallavaṉ*	shi*t*pŭvullŭvŭn
farmer	*vēḷāṇmäikkāraṉ*	vay*l*ah*n*m*ay*kkahrŭn
farrier	*iḷāḍaṅkaṭṭugiṟavaṉ*	ilahdŭng-kuttŭghirrŭvŭn
— (veterinary)	*kuḍiräi-vaittiyaṉ*	kŭ*th*ir*ay*-*v*ith-thiyŭn
fencing-master	*çilamba-vittuvāṉ*	shilŭmbŭ-vith-thuvahn
fruiterer	*kaṉi-viyābāri*	kuni-viyahbahri
fisherman (by caste)	*çempaḍavaṉ*	shempŭdŭvŭn
florist	*pūntōṭṭakkāraṉ*	poon-thoh*t*tŭkkahrŭn
goldsmith	*taṭṭāṉ, poṟkollaṉ*	thuttahn, po*t*kollŭn
grocer	*palaçarakku-viyābā-*	pulŭshurŭkkŭ-viyahbah-
hatter	*toppi-çeygiṟavaṉ* [*ri*	thoppi-sheyghirrŭvŭn [ri
ironmonger	*iruppukkaruvi-viyā-*	irŭppŭkkurŭvi-viyahbah-
jeweller	*nagäi-viyābāri* [*bāri*	nug*ay*-viyahbahri [ri
laundress	*vaṇṇātti*	vu*nn*ahththi
merchant	*varttagaṉ, viyābāri*	vurth-thŭgŭn, viyahbahri
miller	*tirigäikkāraṉ*	thirig*ay*kkahrŭn
milliner	*peṇgaḷiṉ taläikkō-lan-taippavaṉ*	pe*n*gŭlin thul*ay*kkoh-lŭn-thi*p*pŭvŭn
money-changer	*kāçu māṟṟugiṟavaṉ*	kahshŭ mah*tt*ŭghirrŭvŭn
optician (seller)	*kaṇṇādi viyābāri*	ku*nn*ahdi viyahbahri
painter, decorator	*çittirak-kāraṉ*	shiththirŭk-kahrŭn
photographer	*çāyal piḍikkiṟavaṉ*	shahyŭl pidikkirrŭvŭn
policeman	*pōlīs-kāraṉ*	pohlees-kahrŭn
porter (carrier)	*çumäikkāraṉ*	shŭm*ay*kkahrŭn
postmaster	*tapāl-taläivaṉ*	thupahl-thul*ay*vŭn
printer	*accaḍikkiṟavaṉ*	uchchudikkirrŭvŭn
saddler	*çēṇan-taikkiṟavaṉ*	shay*n*ŭn-th*i*kkirrŭvŭn
schoolmaster	*uvāttiyār*	ŭvahth-thiyahr
servant	*vēläikkāraṉ*	vayl*ay*kkahrŭn
shoemaker	*çemmāṉ, çakkiliyaṉ*	shemmahn, shukkiliyŭn
shopkeeper	*kaḍaikkāraṉ*	kud*ay*kkahrŭn
singer	*pāḍagaṉ*	pahdŭgŭn
smith	*kaṇmāḷaṉ*	kummah*lŭn*

English.	Tamil (romanized).	Pronunciation.
soldier	*pōrccēvagaṉ*	pohrch-chayvūgŭn
student	*māṇākkaṉ*	mahnahkkŭn
surgeon	*çattira-vaittiyaṉ*	shuth-thirū-viththiyŭn
surveyor (land)	*nilam-aḷappōṉ*	nilŭm-uluppohn
tailor	*taiyaṭkāraṉ*	thiyutkahrŭn
teacher	*uvātti, upa-dēçi*	ūvahth-thi, ūpŭthayshee
tobacconist	*pugäiyilāi-viyābāri*	pūgayyilay-viyahbahri
tradesman	*varttagaṉ, vaṇigaṉ*	vurth-thūgŭn, vunigŭn
washerman	*vaṇṇāṉ*	vunnahn
watchmaker	*keḍiyārañçeyvōṉ*	ghediyahrŭng-sheyvohn

18. Travelling. (*Pirayāṇam.*)

(For Conversations see pages 49—51.)

Arrival	*varavu, varugäi*	vurŭvū, vurūgay
arrive, to	*vandu çēr*	vundū shayr
bag	*pai, açambi*	pi, ushŭmbi
bill	*kaṇakku, çīṭṭu*	kunŭkkū, sheettū
box, trunk	*peṭṭi*	petti
bridle	*kaḍivāḷam*	kudivahlŭm
cabman	*vaṇḍikkāraṉ, kudi-*	vundikkahrŭn, kūdiraykk-
carriage	*vaṇḍi [räikkāraṉ*	vundi [kahrŭn
coach	*iratam*	iruthŭm
coachman	*irataçārati, tērppā-*	iruthŭshahrūthi, thayrp-
cushion	*mettäi [gaṉ*	meth-thay [pahgŭn
custom-house	*āyatturäi, rēvu*	ahyuth-thūrray, rayvū
custom-house offi-	*āyakkāraṉ*	ahyukkahrŭn
depart, to [cer	*puṟappaḍu, pō*	pūrruppadū, poh
departure	*puṟappāḍu, pōkku*	pūrruppahdū, pohkkū
engine	*iyantiram, çūtti-*	iyunthirŭm, shooth-thi-
expenses	*çelavu [ram*	shelŭvū [rŭm
fare (charge)	*payaṇakkūli*	puyŭnŭkkooli
guard	*kāvalaṉ*	kahvŭlŭn
guide	*vaṟikātti [gam*	vuryi-kahtti [gŭm
guide-book	*vaṟikāṭṭum-pusta-*	vuryi-kahttūm-pūsthū-
hat-box	*toppi-vaikkum-peṭṭi*	thoppi-vikkūm-petti
hotel	*ōṭel, viḍudi*	ohtel, vidūthi
interpreter	*tuppāçi, çuvābnavīs*	thūppahshi, shūvahb-
key	*çāvi*	shahvi [navees
landlady	*ōtel-talāivi*	ohtel-thulayvi
landlord (hotel)	*ōṭel-kāraṉ, -talāivaṉ*	ohtel-kahrŭn, -thulayvŭn

English.	Tamil (romanized).	Pronunciation.
lavatory	*ullarāi*	ūllurray
luggage	*çāmān, tattumuttu*	shahmahn, thuttūmūttū
office	*toril-arāi*	thoryil-urray
payment	*koduttal, çambalam,*	kodūththūl, shumbūlūm,
pier, bridge	*pālam [çellu*	pahlum [shellū
porter	*çumāikkāran*	shumaykkahrūn
railway	*iruppuppādāi*	irūppūpahthay
— -carriage	*reyilvē-vandi*	rayyilvay-vandi
— -station	*reyilvē-stānam*	rayyilvay-sthahnūm
receipt	*pattuccīttu*	puttūch-cheettū
reins	*kadivāla-vār*	kudivahlū-vahr
road	*vari, vīti, pādāi*	vuryi, veethi, pahthay
saddle	*çēnam*	shaynūm [gahrūn
station-master	*(reyilvē) stānādigā-*	(rayyilvay) sthahnahthi-
steamer	*pugāikkappal [ran*	pūgaykkuppūl
strap	*kaccu, vār*	kuch-chū, vahr
ticket	*tundu, çīttu*	thūndū, sheettū
tourist	*payanakkāran*	puyūnūkkahrūn
train (railway)	*vandittodar*	vandith-thodūr
voyage	*kappal-yāttirāi*	kuppūl-yahth-thiray
waiter	*kaiyāl, ēvatkāran*	kiyahl, ayvūtkahrūn
waiting-room	*katt'irukkum arāi*	kahthth'irūkkūm array
whip	*çavukku, kaçāi*	shuvūkkū, kushay

19. Commercial and Trading Terms.

(*Varttagattitkuriya çotkal.*)

(For Conversations see pages 62 & 68.)

English.	Tamil (romanized).	Pronunciation.
Account	*kanakku*	kunūkkū
—, current	*çellun-kanakku*	shellūng-kunūkkū
—, joint	*poduk-kanakku*	pothūk-kunūkkū
—, to close	*kanakku-mudi*	kunūkkū-mudi
—, to settle an	*kanakkut-tīr*	kunūkkūth-theer
— of sale	*vikkirayak-kanakku*	vikkirūyūk-kunūkkū
acknowledgment	*arikkāiyidugāi, kaiç-*	urrikkayyidūgay, ki-ch-
advance (of money)	*mun-panam [çīttu*	mūn-punūm [cheettū
advice, letter	*arikkāippattiram*	urrikkaypputtirūm
agency	*karttattuvam*	kurth-thūth-thūvum
agent	*kāriyakkāran*	kahriyūkkahrūn
apprentice	*toril-payila-v-udan pattavan*	thoryil-puyilū-v-ūdūn puttūvūn

English.	Tamil (romanized).	Pronunciation
arrangement	tiṭṭam-paṇṇudal	thittŭm-punnŭthŭl
arrears	niluvāi, pākki	nilūvay, bahkki
assets	poruḷ, vastu	porūl, vustū
authorize, to	adigāraṅ-koḍu	uthigahrūng-kodū
average	çarāçari	shurahshuri
balance (remain-	niluvāi, kaiyiruppu	nilūvay, kiyirūppū
— -sheet [der)	pākkittāḷ	bahkkith-thahl
bank	bāṅgu, kāçukkaḍāi	bahng-gū, kahshūkkuday
bearer	koṇḍu varugiṟavan	kondū vurūghirrūvūn
bill	kaṇakku-c-cīṭṭu	kunūkkū-ch-cheettū
— of exchange	uṇḍiyaṭ-cīṭṭu	undiyūt-cheettū
— of lading	vārnāmāccīṭṭu	vahrnahmahch-cheettū
bond, in	paṇḍaçālāiyil	pundūshahlayyil
bonded goods	paṇḍaçālāiyil vaitta çāmangaḷ, çēmap-	pundūshahlayyil vith-thū shahmahngūl, shay-
book-keeper	kaṇakkan [poruḷ	kunūkkūn [mūpporūl
brokerage	taragu [bāram	thurūgū [bahrūm
business	vēlāi, kāriyam, viyā-	vaylay, kahriyam, viyah-
buyer	vilāikku vāṅgugiṟa-	vilaykkū vahnggūghirrū-
cargo	kappaṭcarakku [ran	kuppūtchurūkkū [vūn
carriage	çumāi-kūli	shūmay-kooli
— (freight)	ēṟṟumadi, kēḷvu	ayttūmūthi, kaylvū
cartage	vaṇḍiccattam	vundich-chuth-thūm
catalogue	aṭṭavaṇāi, ḍāppu	uttūvunay, dahppū
charter a ship, to	kēḷvukkukkoḍu	kaylvūkkūkkodū
claim	toḍarcci, tāvā	thodūrch-chi, thahvah
clearing-house	āyatturāi, irēvu	ahyuth-thurray, irayvū
clerk [(customs)	kumastā	gūmusthah
commercial traveller	viyāpārattukku pirayāṇakkāran	viyahpahrūth-thūkkū pirūyahnūkkahrūn
company	kūṭṭam, çaṅgam	koottūm, shunggūm
—, a limited	maṭṭuppaṭṭa çaṅgam	muttūpputtū shunggūm
complaint	muṟāippāḍu, pirādu	mūrrayppahdū, pirahthū
contract	uḍanpaḍikkāi	ūdūnpudikkay
cost, insurance and freight (c.i.f.)	vilāiyum uttaravādamum kēḷvum	vilayyum ūth-thūrūvahthūmūm kaylvūm
credit balance	kaiyiruppu	kiyirūppū
creditor	kaḍan koḍuttavan	kudūn kodūth-thūvūn
customs' duties	tīrvāi, āyam, çuṅ-	theervay, ahyūm, shūng-
damages	çēdattin vilāi [gam	shaythūththin vilay [gūm

English.	Tamil (romanised).	Pronunciation.
damages, to claim	*çēdattin vilāi kēḷ*	shay*th*ŭth-thin vil*ay* kay*l*
date, at three months'	*idu mudal mūṉṟu mādattukku*	i*th*ū mū*th*ŭl moonrū mah*th*uththŭkkū
debit and credit	*paṯṯu-varavu*	pu*tt*ū-vurŭvū
debtor	*kaḍaṉ-kāraṉ*	kudŭn-kahrŭn
deed	*çādaṉam*	shah*th*ŭnŭm
deliver, to	*oppukkoḍu* [*koḍutta*	oppŭkkodŭ [kodŭth-thŭ
delivered free	*ilavaçamāy oppuk-*	ilŭvŭshŭmahy oppŭk-
demurrage	*paḍippaṇam*	pudippu*n*um
director	*ēvuvāṉ, talāivaṉ*	ayvŭvahn, thul*ay*vŭn
discount	*taḷḷupaḍi*	thu*ll*ūpudi
—, to	*kuṟāi, kaṟi*	kŭrr*ay*, kuryi
dividend [dues	*pācciyam*	pahch-chiyŭm
dock and harbour	*tuṟāimugattīrvāi*	thŭrr*ay*mūgath-theerv*ay*
drawer (of bill)	*çambiradi, irāyaçaṉ*	shumbirŭ*th*i, irahyŭshŭn
duty, export	*ēṯṯumadittīrvāi*	ay*tt*umu*th*ith-theerv*ay*
— -free	*tīrvāiyillādadu*	theerv*ay*-yillah*th*ŭ*th*ŭ
—, import	*iṟakkumadittīrvāi*	irrukkŭmu*th*ith-theerv*ay*
—, liable to	*tīrvāiyāṉa*	theerv*ay*yahnŭ
enclosed	*aḍāitta, uḷḷiṭṭa*	ud*ay*th-thŭ, u*ll*ittŭ
enclosure	*aḍaippu, aḍakkam*	ud*ay*ppŭ, udŭkkŭm
endorse, to	*çellu-vai*	shellŭ-v*i*
endorsement	*çellu*	shellŭ
exchange (of money)	*vaṭṭam*	vuttŭm [shahl*ay*
factory	*toṟil nadattuñ çālāi*	thoryil nudŭth-thŭ*ng*
the firm	*varttagar-kūṭṭam*	vurth-thŭgŭr-koottŭm
forwarding	*aṉuppum*	unŭppŭm
— agent	*oppaḍāi-çeyvōṉ*	oppud*ay*-sheyvohn
gross weight	*mottamāṉa pāram*	moththŭmahnŭ bahrŭm
guarantee	*uttaravādi*	ŭth-thŭrŭvah*th*i
I.O.U.	*kaḍaṉ çīṭṭu*	kudŭn sheettŭ
import and export	*iṟakkumadiyum ēṯ-*	irrukkŭmu*th*iyŭm ay*tt*ŭ-
income	*varavu* [*ṯumadiyum*	vurŭvŭ [mu*th*iyŭm
information	*çamāçāram*	shumahshahrŭm
insurance	*uttaravādam*	ŭththŭrŭvah*th*ŭm [gŭn
— broker	*uttaravāda-taragaṉ*	ŭththŭrŭvah*th*ŭ-thurŭ-
— company	*nashṭapālaṉa çañ-gam* [*ṉam*	nashtŭpahlŭnŭ shung-gŭm [*th*ŭnŭm
— policy	*uttaravāda-çāda-*	ŭththŭrŭvah*th*ŭ-shah-
— premium	*uttaravāda-paṇam*	ŭththŭrŭvah*th*ŭ-pu*n*ŭm

English.	Tamil (romanized).	Pronunciation.
insure against, to	*uttaravādam paṇṇu*	ūththŭrŭvahthŭm punnŭ
interest	*vaṭṭi*	vutti
lease	*paṭṭā*	puttah
— -holder	*paṭṭādār*	puttahthahr
liabilities	*kaḍamäi*	kudŭmay [ayttŭ
load, to	*çumattu, pāramēṯṯu*	shŭmuththŭ, pahrŭm-
loss	*naṭṭam, kēḍu, pāḍu*	nuttŭm, kaydŭ, pahdŭ
manager	*kāriyakkāraṉ*	kahriyŭkkahrŭn
market	*kaḍäi, çandäi*	kuday, shunthay
—, foreign	*paradēçaccandäi*	purŭthayshŭchchunthay
—, home	*çudēçaccandäi*	shŭthayshŭchchunthay
— -day	*çandäi-kūḍu-nāḷ*	shunthay-koodŭ-nahl
— dues	*kaḍäi-tīrväi* [viläi	kuday-theervay
— price	*nirakku, çandäi-*	nirukkŭ, shunthay-vilay
negotiable, saleable	*çellat-takka, viṯkak-*	shellŭth-thukkŭ, vitkŭk-
order (for goods)	*kēḷvi* [kūḍiṉa	kaylvi [koodinŭ
packing	*kaṭṭudal*	kuttŭthŭl
partnership	*kūṭṭu, paṅguḍäimäi*	koottŭ, pungŭdaymay
payable	*çelutta vēṇḍiya*	shelŭth-thŭ vayndiyŭ
per cent.	*nūṯṯukku* [dam	noottŭkkŭ [thŭm
percentage	*nūṯṯukaṉakkuvigi-*	noottŭkunŭkku vighi-
price	*viläi, nirakku*	vilay, nirukkŭ
— -list	*nirakku-nāmā*	nirukkŭ-nahmah
—, net	*kolviläi*	kolvilay
—, selling	*viṯkiṟa viläi*	vitkirrŭ vilay
—, wholesale	*mottaviläi*	moththŭ-vilay
property	*uḍäimäi, āsti, poruḷ*	udaymay, ahsthi, porŭl
quotation (of price)	*viläikkuṟippu*	vilaykkŭrrippŭ
ready money	*rokkam, kaippaṇam*	rokkŭm, kippunŭm
receipt	*paṯṯuccīṭṭu, kaippaṭṭu* [dam	puttŭchcheettŭ, kipputtŭ [thŭm
registered letter	*padivu-çeyda kāgi-*	puthivŭ-sheythŭ kahghi-
— tonnage	*ḍāppil eṟudi vaitta kappal-pāram*	dahppil eryŭthi viththŭ kuppŭl-bahrŭm
registration fee	*ḍāppiṯ cērkkäi-p-paṇam*	dahppitchayrkkay - p - punŭm
rent	*vāḍagäi*	vahdŭgay
representative	*dūtaṉ, piratikāraṉ*	thoothŭn, pirŭthikahrŭn
retail	*çillaṟäi*	shillurray
—, to sell by	*çillaṟäiyil vil*	shillurrayyil vil

English.	Tamil (romanized).	Pronunciation.
salesman (seller)	*viṯkiṟavaṉ*	vitkirrŭvŭn
settling day	*kadan tīrkkiṟa nāḷ*	kudŭn theerkkirrŭ nahl
share	*paṅgu*	punggŭ
ship, to	*kappalil ēṯṯu*	kuppŭlil ayttŭ
shipping charges	*kappal çelavu*	kuppŭl shelŭvŭ
— house	*kappaliṯ çarakk'ēṯṯu-giṟa viyābārigaḷ*	kuppŭlit shurŭkk'ayttŭ-ghirrŭ viyahbahrigŭl
solvent	*kaḍaṉtīrkkakkūḍiya*	kudŭntheerkkŭkkoodiyŭ
stock	*kaiyirukkiṟa poruḷ*	kiyirŭkkirrŭ porŭl
stock-broker	*taragaṉ*	thurŭgŭn
trade (in general)	*viyābāram* [*vādi*	viyahbahrŭm [vahthi
underwriter	*piṉäiyāḷi, uttara-*	pinayyahli, ŭth-thŭrŭ-
wharf	*ēṯṯ'iṟakkumadi-paṇ-ṇun tuṟäi*	aytt'irrukkŭmuthi-pun-nŭn thŭray
wharfage	*karäi-vāḍagäi*	kuray-vahdŭgay
wholesale	*mottamāy*	moth-thŭmahy

20. Post-office and Telegrams. (*Tapāläikkuṟittu.*)

(For Conversations see page 56, and for Postal Rates see page 96.)

Book post	*pustagam-añcal*	pŭsthŭgŭm-angchŭl
cable (telegraph)	*miṉtapāl, tandi*	min-thupahl, thunthi
cable, to	*miṉ-çeydi-y-aṉuppu*	min-shhaythi-y-unŭppŭ
letter post	*kāgidattapāl*	kahghithuth-thupahl
money order	*tapāl-uṇḍiyal*	thupahl-ŭndiyŭl
newspaper wrapper	*çuṯṯu*	shŭttŭ
parcel post	*çippattapāl*	shippŭth-thupahl
postage paid	*tapālkūli koḍukkap-paṭṭadu*	thupahlkooli kodŭkkŭp-puttŭthŭ
postage stamp	*tapal-muttiräi*	thupahl mŭth-thiray
postal (pillar-) box	*tapāl-peṭṭi,-tūṇ-peṭṭi*	thupahl-petti, -thoonpetti
postman	*tapāṯ-(añcaṯ-) kāraṉ*	thupaht-(ungchŭt-)kah-
postmaster	*tapāl-taläivaṉ*	thupahl-thulayvŭn [rŭn
post-office	*tapāl-vīḍu, -kantōr*	thupahl-veedŭ, -kunthohr
register (a letter), to	*padivu vai*	puthivŭ vi
reply paid	*maṟumoṟiccelavu koḍukkappaṭṭadu*	murrŭmoryich-chelŭvŭ kodŭkkŭpputtŭthŭ
telegraph form	*miṉtapāl kaḍudāçi*	minthupahl kudŭthahshi
— messenger	*miṉtapāl çēvagaṉ*	minthupahl shayvŭgŭn
telephone	*tūrappēçum yanti-*	toorŭppayshŭm yunthi-
to be called for	*kēṭkappaḍa* [*ram*	kaytkŭppudŭ [rŭm

21. Shooting and Fishing. (*Vēṭṭäi-ç-çāmāṉgaḷ.*)

(For Conversations see pages 60—62.)

English.	Tamil (romanized).	Pronunciation.
Axe (hatchet)	*kaikkōḍāli*	kikkohdahli
bait; to bait	*iräi; irät pōḍu*	iray; iray pohdū
bank (of a river)	*karäi, tīram*	kuray, theerŭm
basket	*kūḍäi, paṟi, peṭṭi*	kooday, purri, petti
bite, a	*kaḍi*	kudi
boat	*ōḍam, dōṇi*	ohdŭm, *th*ohni
boat-hook	*ōḍakkokkäi*	ohdŭkkokkay
boatman	*ōḍakkāraṉ*	ohdŭkkahrŭn
boatman's pole	*ōḍakkōl*	ohdŭkkohl
breech (of a gun)	*tubākkippiḍaṅgu*	thūbahkkippidŭng-gū
bullet	*kuṇḍu*	gū*n*dū
caps	*tubākki-vartti*	thūbahkki-vurth-thi
cartridge extractor	*tōṭṭāyiḍukki, tōṭṭāk-*	thohttah-yidŭkki, thoht-
cartridges	*tōṭṭā [kuṟaḍu*	thohttah [tahkkŭrrŭdū
cord (string)	*kayiṟu*	kuyirrū
double-barrelled	*iraṭṭäik-kuṟal*	iruttayk-kūryŭl
file	*aram*	urŭm
fish	*mīṉ, maccam*	meen, muchchŭm
fish, to	*mīṉpiḍi*	meenpidi
fisherman	*mīṉpiḍikkiṟavaṉ*	meenpidikkirrŭvŭn
fishing	*mīṉvēṭṭäi*	meenvayttay
— -basket	*mīṉpaṟi*	meenpurri
— -hook	*tūṇḍil mul*	thoo*n*dil mūl
— -line	*mīṉpiḍikkiṟakayiṟu*	meenpidikkirrŭ kuyirrū
— -rod	*tūṇḍiṟ-kōl, -kambu*	thoo*n*dit-kohl, -kumbū
— -tackle	*mīṉvēṭṭäikkaruvigaḷ*	meenvayttayk-kurūvigŭl
float	*midappu [dil*	mi*th*uppū
fly	*īyuruvam-uḷḷa tūṇ-*	ee-yūrūvŭm-ulla thoo*n*dil
game-bag	*vēṭṭäip-pai*	vayttayp-pi
gun	*tuppākki, tubākki*	thūppahkki, thūbahkki
— (in Ceylon)	*tuvakku [-uṟäi)*	thūvŭkkū [ray)
gun-case	*tuppākkip-peṭṭi (or*	thūppahkkip-petti (-ūr-
gunpowder	*veḍimarundu*	vedimurūn*th*ū
hammer (of gun)	*(tuppākkiyiṉ) kuḍi-*	(thūppahkkiyin) kū*th*iray
knife	*katti [räi*	kuth-thi
matches	*tīkkuccu, tiri*	theekkūchchu, thiri
nail	*āṇi*	ahni
net, casting-	*viccu-valäi*	veechchu-vulay

English.	Tamil (romanized).	Pronunciation.
net, draw-	*karäi-valäi*	kur*ay*-vul*ay*
—, fishing-	*valäi*	vul*ay*
—, large sea-	*kayittu-valäi*	kuyi*tt*ū-vul*ay*
pistol	*pistōl*	pisthohl
revolver	*kaittubākki*	k*i*th-thūbahkki
saw (hand-)	*kai-vāl*	k*i*-vah*l*
screw	*tirug'āṇi*	thirūg'ah*n*i
screwdriver	*tirukki*	thirūkki
sheath	*uṟäi, kūḍu*	ūrr*ay*, koodū
shot	*raväi, çaṉṉam*	ruv*ay*, shunnūm
sport	*vēṭṭäi*	vaytt*ay*
sportsman	*vēṭṭäikkāraṉ*	vaytt*ay*kkahrūn
tools	*karuvi, āyudam*	kurūvi, ahyū*th*ūm

22. Cardinal Numbers.* (*Eṇ-peyar.*)

One	*oṉṟu* (vulg., *oṇṇu*)	ondrū (o*n*nū)
two	*iraṇḍu* („ *reṇḍu*)	iru*n*dū (re*n*dū)
three	*mūṉṟu* („ *mūṇu*)	moondrū (moo*n*ū)
four	*nālu, nāṉyu*	nahlū, nahngū
five	*aindu* (vulg., *añju*)	*i*n*th*ū (u*n*gjū)
six	*āṟu*	ahrrū
seven	*ēṟu*	ayryū
eight	*eṭṭu*	ettū
nine	*oṉbadu*	onbŭ*th*ū
ten	*pattu*	puth-thū
eleven	*padiṉ-oṉṟu*	pu*th*in-ondrū
twelve	*paṉ-ṉ-iraṇḍu*	pun-n-iru*n*dū
thirteen	*padiṉ-mūṉṟu*	pu*th*in-moondrū
fourteen	*padi'ṉālu, padi'ṉāṉgu*	pu*th*i'nahlu, pu*th*i'nahngū
fifteen	*padiṉ-aindu*	pu*th*in-*i*n*th*ū
sixteen	*padiṉ-āṟu*	pu*th*in-ahrrū
seventeen	*padiṉ-ēṟu*	pu*th*in-ayryū
eighteen	*padiṉ-eṭṭu*	pu*th*in-ettū
nineteen	*patt'-oṉbadu*	pathth'onbŭ*th*ū
twenty	*iru-badu, -vadu*	irūbŭ*th*ū, -vŭ*th*ū [th'o*nn*u
twenty-one	*iru-batt'-oṉṟu, iruvatt'*	irūbŭthth'ondrū, irūvŭth-
twenty-two	*irubatt'-iraṇḍu* [*-oṇṇu*	irūbŭthth'iru*n*dū
twenty-three	*irubattu-mūṉṟu*	irūbŭththū-moondrū
thirty	*muppadu*	mūppŭ*th*ū

* For the Tamil signs for the numerals see *Tamil Grammar S.-T.*, pp. 39-41.

English.	Tamil (romanized).	Pronunciation.
forty	*nāṟ-padu*	nah*t*-pŭ*th*ū
fifty	*aim-badu*	*i*m-bŭ*th*ū
sixty	*aṟu-badu*	urrū-bŭ*th*ū
seventy	*eṟu-badu, -vadu*	eryū-bŭ*th*ū, -vŭ*th*ū
eighty	*eṇ-badu*	e*n*-bŭ*th*ū
ninety	*toṇṇūṟu*	tho*nn*oorrū
100	*nūṟu*	noorrū
101	*nūṟṟ' oṉṟu*	noott' ondrū
103	*nūṟṟu mūṉṟu*	noottu moondrū
200	*iru-nūṟu*	irū-noorrū
300	*mu-n-nūṟu*	mū-n-noorrū
400	*nā'-nūṟu*	nah'-noorrū
500	*ain-nūṟu*	*i*n-noorrū
600	*aṟu-nūṟu*	urrū-noorrū
700	*eṟu-nūṟu*	eryu-noorrū
800	*eṇ nūṟu*	e*n*-*n*oorrū
900	*toḷ-ḷ-āyiram*	tho*l*-*l*-ahyirŭm
1,000	*āyiram*	ahyirŭm
1,001	*āyiratt' oṉṟu*	ahyirŭthth'ondrū
1,100	*āyiratt'-oru-nūṟu*	ahyirŭthth'orū-noorrū
2,000	*iraṇḍ' āyiram*	iru*n*d'ahyirŭm
100,000	*ilaṭcam*	ilutchŭm
1906 ...	*ōr-āyirattu-t-toḷ-ḷ-āyiratt'-āṟu*	ohr-ahyiruththu-th-tho*l*-*l*ahyiraththʼahrrū

23. Ordinal Numbers.* (*Eṇṇuriyilakkam.*)

English.	Tamil (romanized).	Pronunciation.
First	*mudal-ām, mudal-āvadu*	mū*th*ŭl-ahm, mū*th*ŭl-ahvŭthū
second	*iraṇḍ'-ām, iraṇḍ'-āvadu*	iru*n*d'-ahm, iru*n*d'-ahvŭ*th*ū
third	*mūṉṟ'-ām*	moondr'-ahm
fourth	*nāl'-ām*	nahl'-ahm
fifth	*aind'-ām*	*i*n*th*'-ahm
sixth	*āṟ'-ām*	ahrr'-ahm
seventh	*ēṟ'-ām*	ayry'-ahm
eighth	*eṭṭ'-ām*	ett'-ahm
ninth	*oṉbad'-ām*	onbŭ*th*'-ahm
tenth	*patt'-ām*	puthth'-ahm
eleventh	*padiṉ-ōr-ām*	pu*th*in-ohr-ahm
twelfth	*paṉṉiraṇḍ'-ām*	punniru*n*d'-ahm

* For Grammatical Notes, see *Tamil Grammar S.-T.*, page 40, para. 20.

English.	Tamil (romanized).	Pronunciation.
thirteenth	*padin-mūnr'-ām*	puthin-moondr'-ahm
fourteenth	*padi'nāl'-ām*	puthi'nahl'-ahm
fifteenth	*padin-aind'-ām*	puthin-inth'-ahm
sixteenth	*padin-ār'-ām*	puthin-ahrr'-ahm
seventeenth	*padin-ēr'-ām*	puthin-ayry'-ahm
eighteenth	*padin-ett'-ām*	puthin-ett'-ahm
nineteenth	*patt'-onbad'-ām*	puthth'-onbŭth'ahm
twentieth	*irubad'-ām*	irūbŭth'-ahm
twenty-first	*irubatt'-ōr-ām*	irūbŭthth'-ohr-ahm
twenty-second	*irubatt'-irand'-ām*	irūbŭthth'-irŭnd'-ahm
thirtieth	*muppad'-ām*	mūppŭth'-ahm
fortieth	*nātpad'-ām*	nahtputh'-ahm
fiftieth	*aimbad'-ām*	imbŭth'-ahm
sixtieth	*arubad'-ām*	urrūbŭth'-ahm
seventieth	*erubad'-ām*	eryubŭth'-ahm
eightieth	*enbad'-ām*	enbŭth'-ahm
ninetieth	*tonnūr'-ām*	thonnoorr'-ahm
100th	*nūr'-ām*	noorr'-ahm
101st	*nūtt'ōr-ām*	noott'ohr-ahm
102nd	*nūtt'-irand'-ām*	noott'-irund'ahm
200th	*iru-nūr'-ām*	irū-noorr'-ahm
300th	*munnūr'-ām*	mūn-noorr'-ahm
1000th	*āyiram-ām*	ahyirŭm-ahm
1001st	*āyiratt'-ōr-ām*	ahyirŭthth'-ohr-ahm

24. Collective Numbers, etc. (*Togudippeyargaḷ.*)

A couple, pair	*jōdu, iṇäi, tuṇäi*	johdū, inay, thūnay
double, twice *adj.*	*irattäiyana, irukal*	iruttayyahnŭ, irukahl
dozen	*pannirandu*	punnirundū
one-fifth	*nāngu mā** / *aindil onru*	nahngū-mah / inthil ondrū
half	*aräi*	uray
once	*oru-viçäi, orumuräi*	orū-vishay, orūmūrray
quarter	*kāl*	kahl
score	*irubadu*	irūbŭthū
single	*ottäi*	ottay
one-third	*mūnril onru*	moondril ondrū
three-quarters	*mukkāl*	mūkkahl
two and a half	*irand'aräi*†	irunduray

* See Grammar, sec. 22.

† See Grammar, sec. 22, note.

CONVERSATIONAL PHRASES AND SENTENCES.

Useful & Necessary Idiomatic Expressions & Phrases.

(*Pirayōjaṉamuḷḷa vaṟakkanaḍäiyāṉa vārttäigaḷum vākkiyaṅgaḷum.*)

English.	Tamil (romanized).	Pronunciation.
Thank you:		
(To servants)	*nalladu*	nullŭthū
(To equals and superiors)	*umakku-t-tōttiram* / *umakku vandaṉam*	ūmŭkkūth-thohththirūm / ūmŭkkū vunthŭnūm
I thank you	*umakku naṉṟi çollugiṟēṉ*	ūmŭkkū nundri shollūghirrayn
Have the goodness	*naṉmäiyāy irukkavum; tayavu-paṇṇum*	nunmayyahy irūkkŭvūm; thuyŭvū punnūm
Yes, sir	*ām, aiyā*	ahm, iyah
No, madam	*illäi, ammā (turäiçāṉi)*	illay, ummah (thūray-shahni)
Yes, miss	*ām, turäimagaḷ*	ahm, thūray-mugŭl
Bring me	*eṉakku-k-koṇḍu vā*	enŭkkū-k-kondū vah
Do you understand?	*uṉakku-t-teriyum-ā?*	ūnŭkkū-th-theriyūm-ah?
Excuse me	*eṉṉäi maṉṉiyum*	ennay munniyūm
Give me	*eṉakku-k-koḍu*	enŭkkū-k-kodū
Send (it) to me	*eṉakku (adäi) aṉuppu*	enŭkkū (uday) unūppū
Tell me	*eṉakku-c-collu*	enŭkkŭ-ch-chollū
Will you tell me?	*eṉakku-c-colluvīr-ā?*	enŭkkū-ch-chollūveer-ah?
Do you speak English?	*iṅgilish pēçugiṟīr-ā?*	inglhilish payshūghir-reer-ah?
Does anyone here speak English?	*ing'irukkum evar-āyilum iṅgilish pēçugiṟār-ā?*	inggh'irūkkūm evŭr ah-ghilūm inggbilish pay-shūghirrahr-ah?
Can you read English?	*uṉakku iṅgilish vāçikka-k-kūḍumā?*	ūnŭkkū inggbilish vah-shikkŭk-koodūm-ah?
Have patience	*poṟumäiyāy iru*	porrūmay-yahy irū?
What do you say?	*nī eṉṉa çollugiṟāy?*	nee ennū shollūghirrahy?
I beg your pardon	*umadu maṉṉippu vēṇḍugiṟēṉ*	ūmŭthū munnippū vayn-dūghirrayn
What did you ask?	*nī eṉṉa kēṭṭāy?*	nee ennū kayttahy?
Speak louder	*iṉṉam urakka-p-pēçu*	innūm ūrukkŭ-p-payshu

English.	Tamil (romanized).	Pronunciation.
What does it signify?	*adu eṉṉattäi-k-karudugiṟadu?*	uthū ennŭththayk-kurūthūghirrŭthū?
It doesn't matter	*adu kāriyam alla*	uthū kahriyūm ullū
It is all the same to me	*ellām eṉakku-c-cari tāṉ*	ellahm enŭkkū-ch-churi thahn
Never mind	*kāriyam illäi*	kahriyūm illay
What is to be done?	*eṉṉa çeyya vēṇḍiyadu?*	ennū sheyyŭ vayndiyŭthū?
Do you hear?	*kēṭkiṟīr-ā?*	kaytkirreer-ah?
I understand	*eṉakku-t-teriyum; aṟigiṟēṉ*	enŭkkū-th-theriyūm; urrighirrayn
I don't understand	*eṉakku-t-teriyādu; aṟiyēṉ*	enŭkkū-th-theriyahthū; urriyayn
Carry this	*idäi-k-koṇḍu pō*	ithay-k-kondū poh
Take this	*idäi-y-edu*	ithay-y-edū
Take this away	*idäi-y-eḍuttu-k-koṇḍu pō*	ithay-y-edūththū-k-kondū poh
Why are you so slow?	*nī ēṉ appaḍi mandamāy irukkiṟāy?*	nee ayn uppŭdi munthŭmahy irukkirrahy?
Make haste!	*viräiv 'ākku!*	virayv'ahkkū!
Come along!	*kūḍa vā! neḍuga vā!*	koodŭ vah! nedūgū vah!
Take care!	*kavaṉamāy iru!*	kuvŭnūmahy irū!
Look out!	*eccarikkäiyāy iru!*	echchurikkayyahy iru!
Listen!	*uṭṭu-k-kēḷ!*	ūttū-k-kayl!
Come in!	*uḷḷē vā!*	ūllay vah!
Come here!	*iṅgē vā!*	ing-gay vah!
Come back!	*tirumbi vā!*	thirūmbi vah!
Call my servant	*eṉ çēvaganäi-k-kūpiḍu*	en shayvŭgŭnay-k-koopidū
Take this note	*inda çīṭṭäi-y-eḍu*	intha sheettay-yedū
Bring an answer	*uttaram koṇḍu vā*	uththŭrūm kondū vah
Stand still	*amäidiyāy nil*	umaythiyahy nil
Go away!	*pōy viḍu!*	pohy vidū!
That way	*anda vaṟiyāy; appaḍi*	unthŭ vuryiyahy; uppudi
This way	*inda vaṟiyāy; ippaḍi*	inthŭ vuryiyahy; ippudi
Too soon	*mikka çīkkiramāy*	mikkū sheekkirūmahy
Too late	*miga-p-pindi*	migŭ-p-pinthi
Very well	*migavum nalladu*	migŭvūm nullŭthū
What do you want?	*uṉakku eṉṉa vēṇḍum?*	ūnŭkkū yennŭ vayndūm?
Will you do me a favour?	*nīr eṉakku oru çahāyam çeyvīr-ā?*	neer enŭkkū orū suhahyūm sheyveer-ah?
What is it?	*adu eṉṉa?*	uthū ennū?

English.	Tamil (romanized).	Pronunciation.
I am very much obliged to you	*nāṉ umakku adiya kaḍamäiyuḷḷava-ṉāy irukkiṟēṉ*	nahn ūmŭkkū u*th*igŭ kudŭm*ayūll*ŭvŭnahy irūkkirrayn
I shall be much obliged to you	*nāṉ umakku miga-vum kaḍamäiyuḷ-ḷavaṉāy iruppēṉ*	nahn ūmŭkkū migŭvūm kudŭm*ayūll*ŭvŭnahy irūppayn
I am sorry to trouble you so much	*umakku ivvaḷav'āy tondaravu paṇṇu-giṟadaṯku eṉakku tukkam uṇḍu*	ūmŭkkū ivvŭlŭvahy thon-*th*ūrŭvū pu*nn*ūghirrŭ-*th*ŭ*t*kū (y)enŭkkū tūk-kŭm ŭndū
No trouble at all	*tondaravu koñja-mum illäi*	thon*th*ūrŭvū ko*ng*jŭmūm ill*ay*
What is the matter with you?	*uṉakku eṉṉa varut-tam* (or *kāriyam*)?	ūnŭkkū ennŭ vurūth-thŭm (kahriyŭm)?
What is the matter?	*eṉṉa kāriyam?*	ennŭ kahriyŭm?
Nothing	*oṉṟum illäi*	ondrūm ill*ay*
Who is there?	*aṅgē yār?*	unggay yahr?
It is I	*nāṉ tāṉ*	nahn thahn
What is the news?	*çaṅgadi eṉṉa?*	shunggŭ*th*i ennŭ?
Have you any news?	*uṉakku ēdum çeydi uṇḍā?*	ūnŭkkū ay*th*ūm shey*thi* ŭndah?
I have heard nothing	*nāṉ oṉṟum kēṭṭ'-irukka-v-illäi*	nahn ondrūm kaytt'irūk-kŭ-v-ill*ay*
Are you quite certain?	*uṉakku muṟudum niccayam-ā?*	ūnŭkkū mūryū*th*ūm nichchŭyŭm-ah?
What has happened?	*eṉṉa çambavitt' irukkiṟadu?*	ennŭ shumbŭviththʼ-irukkirrŭ*th*ū?
What temple is that?	*adu eṉṉa kōvil?*	u*th*ū ennŭ kohvil?
Begone! *or* Go!	*pō!*	poh!
Go away from here	*ivviḍam viḍu-p-pōy*	ivvidŭm vittū-p-pohy
Go on (continue)	*iḍäi viḍāmal çey*	id*ay* vidahmŭl shey
Go home	*vīṭṭukku-p-pō*	veettŭkkū-p-poh
Go to the post-office and bring me the letters	*tabāl çāvadikku-p-pōy eṉ kāgidaṅ-galäi-k-koṇḍu vā*	thubahl shahvŭdikkū-p-pohy kahghi*th*ŭnggu-l*ay*k-kondū vah
Show me the house of the Consul	*stānāpati-vīṭṭäi eṉakku-k-kāṭṭu*	sthahnahputhi-veett*ay* (y)enŭkkū-k-kahttū
Let us start	*puṟappaḍuvōm*	pūrruppudūvohm
Get everything ready	*ellām āyattam paṇ-ṇu*	ellahm ahyūththŭm pu*nn*u

Note: "[vidu" / "[vidū" appear as bracketed continuations of "Go away from here" entries (*viḍu*, vidū).

English.	Tamil (romanized).	Pronunciation.
Wait; (stay)	*kātt'iru; (poṟu)*	kahthth'irū; (porru)
Here I am	*nāṉ iṅgē irukkiṟēṉ*	nahn inggay yirūkkirrayn
Be good enough to tell me	*eṉakku-c-colla naṉmäiyāy irum*	enŭkkū-ch-chollŭ nunmayyahy irūm
Hear what I tell you	*nāṉ uṉakku-c-collugiṟadäi-k-kēl*	nahn ŭnŭkkū-ch-chollūghirrŭthay-k-kayl
Bring me my horse	*eṉ kudiräiyäi-k-kondu vā*	(y)en kuthirayyay-k-kondū vah
Speak with the interpreter	*tuvibāshigaṉōdu pēçu*	thūvibahshigunohdū payshū
Speak to him	*avaṉukku-p-pēçu*	uvŭnŭkkū-p-payshū
What does this mean?	*idu eṉṉattäi-k-karudugiṟadu?*	ithu ennŭththay-k-kurūthūghirrŭthū?

Expressions of Emotions.

(*Maṉōçalaṉam kāṭṭugiṟa vārttäigaḷ.*)

What?	*eṉṉa?*	ennŭ?
Is it possible?	*ēlumā?*	(y)aylūmah?
Indeed!	*meyyāgavē!*	meyyahgŭvay!
That is impossible	*adu ēlādu*	uthū (y)aylahthū
That cannot be	*adu irukkamāṭṭādu* (or *kūḍādu*)	uthū irūkkŭ mahttahthū (koodahthū)
You surprise me	*nī eṉṉäi atiçayippikkiṟāy*	nee ennay uthishuyippikkirrahy
Don't touch	*toḍādē*	thodahthay
My fault	*eṉ kuṭṭam; eṉ tappu*	en kūttŭm; en thuppū
Oh! it's nothing	*ā! adu kāriyam alla*	ah! uthū kahriyŭm ullŭ
I am sorry for it	*nāṉ adaṟkāga tukkamāy irukkiṟēṉ*	nahn uthŭtkahgū thūkkŭmahy irūkkirrayn
I am quite vexed about it	*nāṉ adäi-k-kuṟittu muṟudum aläiccal paṭṭ'irukkiṟēṉ*	nahn uthay-k-kūrriththū mūryūthūm ulaychchŭl putt'irūkkirrayn
What a pity!	*evvaḷavu irakkam!*	evvŭlŭvū irukkŭm!
It is a sad thing	*adu tukkamāṉa kāriyam*	uthū thūkkŭmahnŭ kahriyŭm
Bravo!	*çabāçu!*	shubahshū!
Well done!	*naṉṟāy muḍindadu!*	nundrahy mūdinthŭthū!
How fortunate!	*evvaḷavu atishṭam!*	evvŭlŭvū utheeshtŭm!
How beautiful!	*evvaḷavu aṟagu!*	evvŭlŭvū uryŭgū!
All right!	*ellāñ çari!*	ellahng shuri!
I am very glad	*nāṉ migavum çantōçamāy irukkiṟēṉ*	nahn migŭvŭm shunthohshŭmahy irūkkirrayn
How shocking!	*evvaḷavu koḍumäi!*	evvŭlŭvū kodūmay!

English.	Tamil (romanized).	Pronunciation.
He is very angry	*avan migavum kōpa-māy irukkirān*	uvŭn migŭvŭm kohpŭ-mahy irūkkirrahn
What a shame!	*evvaḷavu vetkakkēḍu!*	evvŭlŭvŭ vetkŭkkaydŭ!
How could you do so?	*nī avvidam eppaḍi-c-ceydāy?*	nee uvvithŭm eppudi-ch-chaythahy?
I am ashamed of you	*nān unnäi-k-kurittu vetka-p-paḍugirēn*	nahn ŭnnay-k-kŭrriththŭ vetkŭ-p-pudŭghirrayn
For shame!	*çī çī!*	shee shee!
You are very much to blame	*nī migavum kuṭṭat-tukk' utpaṭṭaran-āy irukkirāy*	nee migŭvŭm kŭttŭth-thŭkk'ŭtputtŭvŭnahy irūkkirrahy
Hold your tongue!	*un vāy mūḍu!*	ŭn vahy moodŭ!

Notices. (*Arikkäigaḷ.*)

English.	Tamil (romanized).	Pronunciation.
Apartments	*vīṭṭin aṟäigaḷ*	veettin urraygŭl
Entrance	*vāçal; durāram*	vashŭl; thŭvahrŭm
Exit	*puṟappaḍum vaṟi*	pŭrruppudŭm vuryi
Fire alarm	*tī-y-accakkuṟippu*	thee-y-uchchŭkkŭrrippŭ
Furnished rooms	*jōḍitta aṟäigaḷ*	johdiththŭ urraygŭl
Keep off the grass	*pullanäi-mēl varā-mal naḍa*	pŭllunay-mayl vurahmŭl nudŭ
Knock; ring	*taṭṭu; maṇi-y-aḍi*	thuttŭ; muni-y-udi
No admittance	*utpiravēçikka utta-rav' illäi*	ŭtpirŭvayshikkŭ ŭttŭr ŭv'illay
No smoking allowed	*pugäi-y-iläi kuḍik-kiṟadaṭku uttarav'*	pŭgay-yilay kŭdikkirrŭ-thŭtkŭ ŭththŭrŭv'illay
No thoroughfare	*vaṟi-y-illäi* [*illäi*	vuryi-y-illay
Please do not touch	*toḍādēyum*	thodahthayyum
Please wipe your feet	*umadu pādaṅgaḷäi tuḍäikka-t-tayäi çeyyum*	ŭmŭthŭ pahthŭnggŭlay thŭdaykkŭ-th-thuyay sheyyŭm
Private	*irahaçiyamāna*	iruhŭshiyŭmahnŭ
Public notice!	*piraçitta viḷamba-*[*ram*	pirŭshiththŭ vilumbŭ-[rŭm
Pull; push	*iṟu; taḷḷu*	iryŭ; thullŭ
Refreshments	*āhāram*	ahhahrŭm
To be let, to let	*vāḍagäikku viḍa-p-paḍa*	vahdŭgaykkŭ vidŭ-p pudŭ
To be sold	*viṟka-p-paḍa*	vitkŭ-p-pudŭ
Unfurnished rooms	*jōḍiyāda aṟäigaḷ*	johdiyahthu urraygŭl
Walk in	*uḷḷē naḍa*	ŭllay nudŭ

The Railway. (*Iruppu-p-pādäi.*)

(See Vocabulary 18, page 34.)

English.	Tamil (romanized).	Pronunciation.
To the station	*reyilvē stāṉattukku*	reyilvay sthahnūththūk- [kū
Here is my luggage	*eṉ payaṉac-cāmāṉ iṅgē-y-irukkiṟadu*	en puyūnū-ch-chahmahn inggay-y-irūkkirrū*th*ū
Take it to the cloak-room	*çāmāṉ-aṟäikku adäi eḍuttu-k-koṇḍu-pō*	shahmahn-urr*ay*kkū u*th*-*ay* edūththū-k-ko*n*dū poh
I wish to register my luggage for...	*nāṉ eṉ payaṇa-c-cāmāṉäi ...... ku-p-padivu çeyya virumbugiṟēṉ*	nahn en puyūnū-ch-chah-mahn*ay* ... kū-p-pu*th*ivū sheyyū virūmbūgghirrayn
The luggage is over weight	*payaṇa-c-cāmāṉ niṟäikk'adigam*	puyūnū-ch-chahmahn nirr*ay*kk'a*th*igūm
Get my luggage; here is the ticket	*eṉ çāmāṉäi eḍuttu-k-koṇḍu vā; idu tān tuṇḍu* (or *tikket iṅgē*)	en shahmahn*ay* edūth-thū-k-ko*n*dū vah; i*th*ū thahn thū*n*dū (tikket inggay)
Where is the waiting-room?	*kātt' irukkum aṟäi eṅgē?*	kahthth' irūkkūm urr*ay* enggay?
— is the booking-office?	*padivu çeyyum* (or (*payaṇa-t-tuṇḍu viṟkum*) *çālāi eṅgē?*	pu*th*ivū sheyyūm (puyū*n*aththū*n*dū vi*t*kūm) shahl*ay* enggay?
— is the buffet?	*āhāra stāṉam eṅgē?*	ahhahrū sthahnūm eng- [gay?
— is the lavatory?	*karuvugiṟa aṟäi eṅ-gē?*	kuryūvūghirrū urr*ay*eng-gay?
— is the train [for...?	*...-kku vaṇḍi-t-toḍar* [*eṅgē?*	...-kkū vu*n*di-th-thodūr [enggay?
Are you going by the express?	*viçēshagati vaṇḍi-t-toḍar-variyāy-p-pōgiṟīrā?*	vishayshūguthi vu*n*di-th-thodūr-vuryiyahy-p-pohghir-reerah?
Show me a time-table	*eṉakku nēram-aṭṭa-vaṇäi-k-kāṭṭu*	enūkkū nayrūm-uttūvū-*nay*-k-kahttū
When does the train start?	*reyil vaṇḍi-t-toḍar eppō puṟappaḍum?*	reyil vu*n*di-th-thodūr eppoh pūrruppudūm?
Can I book through to...?	*... -kku nērāy payaṇam pōga tuṇḍu vāṅga-k-kūḍum-ā?*	...-kkū nay-rahy puyū*n*ūm pohgū thū*n*dū vahng-gū-k-koodūm-ah?
A first- (second-) class single ticket to...	*...-kku mudal (iraṇ-ḍām) vaguppu taṉi-t-tuṇḍu* [*dugal*	...-kkū mū*th*ūl (iru*n*-dahm) vugūppū thu*n*i-th-thū*n*dū [gū*l*
Return tickets	*tirumbi varum tuṇ-*	thirūmbi vurūm thū*n*dū-

English.	Tamil (romanized).	Pronunciation.
How much is it?	*adu evvaḷavu ?* *vilāi eṉṉa ?*	uthū evvŭlŭvū ? vilay ennŭ ?
We want a sleeping carriage	*namakkū nittirāi çeygiṟa vaṇḍi vēṇum*	numŭkkū niththiray sheyghirrū vundi vaynūm
A corridor carriage	*oru çuṭṭuccālāi vaṇḍi*	orū shŭttūchchahlay vundi
A carriage for ladies	*turāiçāṉigaḷukku oru vaṇḍi*	thūrayshahnigŭlŭkkū orū vundi
A non-smoking compartment	*çuruṭṭu-k-kuḍiyāda vaṇḍi*	shūrūttū-k-kūdiyahthŭ vundi
Is this the train for...?	*...-kku-p-pōgiṟa vaṇḍi-t-toḍar idu tāṉā ?*	...-kkū-p-pohghirrū vundith-thodŭr ithū thahnah ?
Do I change anywhere on the journey?	*payaṇattil evviḍattilēṉum māṟa vēṇḍumā ?*	puyŭnŭththil evvidŭththilaynūm mahrrŭ vayndūmah ?
Where must I change for...?	*... -kku evviḍattil māṟa vēṇḍum ?*	...... -kkū evvidŭththil mahrrŭ vayndūm ?
Is this seat engaged?	*inda āçaṉam ēṭpaṭṭ' irukkiṟadā ?*	inthū ahshŭnūm aytputt' irūkkirrŭthah ?
There is no room	*iḍam illāi*	idūm illay
Call the guard	*kāvaṭkāraṉāi-k-kūppiḍu*	kahvŭtkahrŭnay-k-kooppidū
The train is just going to start	*vaṇḍi-t-toḍar ippō puṟappaḍa-p-pōgiṟadu*	vundi-thodŭr ippoh pūrrŭppudŭ-p-pohghirrŭthū
Open the door	*kadavāi-t-tiṟa*	kuthŭvay-th-thirrŭ
— the window	*jaṉalāi-t-tiṟa*	junŭlay-th-thirrŭ
Here is the station	*taṅgal stāṉam iṅgē-y-irukkiṟadu*	thunggŭl sthahnūm inggay-y-irŭkkirrŭthū
Do we stop here?	*iṅgē taṅgugiṟōmā ?*	inggay thunggūghirrohmah ?
Do we alight here?	*nāṅgaḷ iṅgē iṟaṅgugiṟōmā?*	nahnggŭl inggay irrunggūghirrohmah?
Do we change carriages here?	*iṅgē nāṅgaḷ vaṇḍi maṭṭugiṟōmā ?*	inggay nahnggŭl vundi mahttūghirrohmah
How long do we stop here?	*nāṅgaḷ evvaḷavu nēram ivviḍattil taṅgi-y-irukkiṟōm*	nahnggŭl evvŭlŭvū nayrūm ivvidŭththil thungghi-y-irūkkirrohm ?
Five minutes	*aindu nimiçam*	inthū nimishūm

English.	Tamil (romanized).	Pronunciation.
My luggage is lost	*eṉ payaṇa-c-cāmāṉ tavaṟi-p-pōy irukkiṟadu*	en puyŭ*n*ŭ-ch-chahmahn thuvŭrri-p-pohy irūkkirrŭ*th*ū
When it arrives, forward it on to...	*adu vandu çērum pōdu ...-kku adäi aṉuppu* [*k-koḍu*	u*th*ū vun*th*ū shayrŭm poh*th*ŭ ...-kkŭ u*thay* unūppū [kodū
Give me your ticket	*uṉ tuṇḍäi eṉakku-*	ūn thū*n*d*ay* enŭkkū-k-
Here it is	*adu iṅgē* (*irukkiṟadu*)	u*th*ū inggay (irūkkirrŭ*th*ū)

The Hotel. (*Çāvaḍi.*)

(See Vocabularies 12—16, pages 26—32.)

English.	Tamil (romanized).	Pronunciation.
Which is the best hotel?	*uttamamāṉa çāvaḍi edu?*	ūththŭmŭmahnŭ shahvŭdi e*th*ū?
Let us have supper soon	*eṅgaḷukku irā-c-cāppāḍu çīkkiramāy koḍu*	enggŭ*l*ūkkū irahchchahppahdū sheekkirŭmahy kodū
Are our rooms ready?	*eṅgaḷ aṟäigaḷ āyattamāy irukkiṉṟaṉā?*	enggŭ*l* urr*ay*gŭ*l* ahyŭththŭmahy irūkkindrŭnah
I want a bedroom	*eṉakku oru paḍukkäi-y-aṟäi vēṇḍum*	enŭkkū orū pudŭkk*ay*-y-urr*ay* vay*n*dūm
Let me see the room	*nān aṟäiyäi-p-pārkkaṭṭum*	nahn urr*ay*y*ay*-p-pahrkkuttūm
What is the price of this room?	*inda aṟäikku viläi-y-eṉṉa?* [*ki*	in*th*ŭ urr*ay*kkū vil*ay*-y-ennŭ?
That is too dear	*adu migavum kirāk-*	u*th*ū migŭvūm kirahkki
I want a cheaper one	*eṉakkū malivāṉad' oṉṟu vēṇum*	enŭkkū mulivahnŭ*th*' ondrū vaynūm
Have you a double-bedded room?	*iraṭṭäi-p-paḍukkäi-y-uḷḷa aṟäi-y-irukkiṟadā?*	irutt*ay*-p-pudūkk*ay*-yū*ll*ŭ urr*ay*-y-irūkkirrŭ*th*ah?
Are there any letters for me?	*eṉakku kāgidaṅgaḷ uṇḍā?* [*eṅgē?*	enŭkkū kahghi*th*ŭnggŭ*l* ŭ*n*dah? [enggay?
Where is the w.c.?	*dabilyu çī uḷḷaṟäi*	dubilyū shee ū*ll*urr*ay*
Can I have a warm bath?	*vennīr snāṉam kiḍäikkumā?*	venneer snahnŭm kid*ay*kkūmah?
Give me the key of my room	*eṉ aṟäi-c-cāviyäi-k-koḍu*	en urr*ay*-ch-chahviy*ay*k-kodū?
Bring me some warm water	*eṉakku koñjam vennīr koṇḍu vā*	enŭkkū ko*ng*jŭm venneer ko*n*dū vah

English.	Tamil (romanized).	Pronunciation.
Take my luggage down	*en payaṉa-c-cāmā-ṉäi-k-kīṟē eḍu*	en puyŭnu-ch-chahmah-nay keeryay edū
Give me a candle, please	*tayavāga eṉakku oru meṟugu vartti koḍum*	thuyuvahgŭ enŭkkū orū meryŭgū vurththi kodūm
We leave early to-morrow morning	*nāḷäi atikāläiyil pōgiṟōm*	nahlay uthikahlayyil pohghirrohm
Call me at seven	*ēḻu maṇikku eṉṉäi-k-kūppiḍu*	(y)ayryū munikkū ennay-k-kooppidū

Breakfast. (*Kālāiccāppāḍu.*)

(See Vocabularies 12 & 13, pages 26—28.)

English.	Tamil (romanized).	Pronunciation.
Is breakfast ready?	*kāläi bōjaṉam āyat-tappaṭṭadā?*	kahlay bohjŭnŭm ahyŭth-thŭpputtŭthah?
Breakfast is ready	*— — āyattappaṭṭa-[du*	– – ahyŭththŭpputtŭthū
Is the tea made?	*tē-nīr muḍind' irukkiṟadā?*	thay-neer mūdinth' irūk-kirrŭthah?
Do you drink...?	*nī...kuḍikkiṟāyā?*	nee...kūdikkirrahy-ah?
This cream is sour	*inda-p-pālāḍäi pu-ḷippāy irukkiṟadu*	indū-p-pahlahday pūlip-pahy irūkkirrŭthū
Will you take...?	*nī...çāppiḍuvāyā?*	nee...shahppidūvahyah?
These eggs are hard	*inda muṭṭäigaḷ kaḍi-ṉam*	inthŭ mūttaygŭl kudi-nŭm
Give me the salt	*uppu eṉakku-k-koḍu*	ūppū enŭkkū-k-kodū
Pass me...	*... eṉakk' aṉuppu*	...enŭkk' unūppū
This butter is not fresh	*inda veṇṇey pudid' alla [du vā*	inthŭ venney pūthith' ullŭ [vah
Bring some more	*koñjam adigam koṇ-*	kongjŭm uthigŭm kondū
Is the coffee strong enough?	*inda-k-kāppi pōdiya pelamāy irukkiṟadā?*	inthŭ-k-kahppi pohthiyŭ pelŭmahy irūkkirrŭthah
We want more cups	*eṅgaḷukku iṉṉum adigam kappi-pāttiram vēṇḍum*	enggŭlŭkkū innūm uthi-gŭm kuppi-pahththi-rŭm vayndūm
Take some more...	*iṉṉum koñjam eḍu*	innūm kongjŭm edū
A piece of toast	*oru tuṇḍu çūḍu-kāt-tiṉa roṭṭi [tuṇḍu*	orū thŭndū shoodū-kaht-tinŭ rotti [thŭndū
A rasher of bacon	*uppiṭṭa paṉṟi-vaṟṟal*	ūppittŭ pandri-vuttŭl
Coffee with milk	*pālōḍu kāppi*	pahlohdū kahppi
Coffee without milk or cream	*pāl, pālāḍäi-y-illā-da kāppi*	pahl, pahlahday-y-illah-thŭ kahppi
Remove the things	*poruṭkaḷäi nīkku*	porūtkŭlay neekkū

Dinner. (*Tiṉi.*)

(See Vocabularies 12 & 13, pages 26—28.)

English.	Tamil (romanized).	Pronunciation.
Show me the bill-of-fare	*çāppāṭṭukku iḍāppu kāṭṭu*	shahppahttūkkū idahppū kahttū
What have you ready?	*uṉṉiḍam āyattamāy irukkiṟad' eṉṉa?*	ūnnidūm ahyuththū-mahy irūkkirrūth' ennu?
What soup will you have?	*uṉakku eṉṉa çūp viruppam?*	ūnūkkū ennū shoop virūppūm?
Have you any...?	*uṉṉiḍam yādēṉum ...irukkiṟadā?*	ūnnidūm yahthaynūm... irūkkirrūthah?
May I give you some fish?	*nāṉ umakku koñjam mīṉ koḍukkalāmā?*	nahn ūmūkkū kongjūm meen kodūkkūlahmah?
Fried soles	*poritta nākku-mīṉ*	poriththū nahkkū-meen
What wine will you have?	*eṉṉa uvayiṉ umakku viruppam?*	ennū ūvuyin ūmūkkū virūppūm?
Here is the list	*iḍāppu iṅgē (irukkiṟadu)*	idahppū inggay (irūkkirrūthū)
We shall dine at three o'clock	*mūṉṟu maṇikku-c-cāppiḍuvōm*	moondrū munikkū-ch-chahppidūvohm
Are you hungry or thirsty?	*paçiyāy alladu dāhamāy irukkiṟīra?*	pushiyahy ullūthū thah-hūhmahy irūkkirreerah?
I am very thirsty	*eṉakku metta dāham eḍukkiṟadu*	enūkkū meththū thah-hūm edūkkirrūthū
What shall I help you to?	*nāṉ uṉakku eṉṉa koḍukka vēṇḍum?*	nahn ūnūkkū ennū ko-dūkkū vayndūm?
Which do you prefer?	*uṉakku edu piriyam?*	ūnūkkū ethū piriyūm?
No, thank you	*vēṇḍām, umakku stuti*	vayndahm, ūmūkkū sthūthi
Help yourself	*umakkē eḍum*	umūkkay edūm
I prefer it well-done	*naṉṟāy ākkiṉadu eṉakku piriyam*	nundrahy ahkkinūthū enūkkū piriyūm
It is excellent	*adu mēlāṉadu*	uthū maylahnūthū
Change the plates	*pīṅgāṉāi māṭṭū*	peenggahnay mahttū
Give me a clean fork	*eṉakku çuttiyāṉa mullu koḍu*	enūkkū shūththiyahnū mūllū kodū
A clean knife	*çuttiyāṉa katti*	shūththiyahnū kuththi
Bring me a glass of water	*eṉakku oru gilās taṇṇīr koṇḍu vā*	enūkkū orū ghilahs thunneer kondū vah
Give me something to drink	*kuḍikka edēṉum koḍu*	kūdikkū ethaynūm kodū
This wine is flat	*inda uvayin-çuvāi-y-aṭṭadu*	inthū ūvuyin-shūvay-y-uttūthū

Tea. (*Tē-nīr.*)

(See Vocabularies 12 & 13, pages 26—28)

English.	Tamil (romanized).	Pronunciation.
Tea is ready	*tē-nīr āyattamāy irukkiṟadu*	thay-neer ahyuththŭ-mahy irūkkirrŭ*th*ū
Will you come?	*varuvīrā?*	vurūveerah?
Pour out the tea	*tē-nīr ūṯṯu*	thay-neer oo*tt*ū
Bring a saucer	*oru taṭṭāippāttiram koṇḍu vā*	orū thutt*ay*ppahththirūm ko*n*dū vah
Ring, if you please	*nī virumbiṉāl maṇi-y-adi*	nee virūmbinahl mu*n*i-y-udi
A little more milk	*koñjam adigam pāl*	ko*ng*jūm u*th*igūm pahl
More bread	*iṉṉam adigam urotti (kodu)*	innūm u*th*igūm ūrotti (kodū)
A slice of bread and butter	*oru tuṇḍu roṭṭiy-um veṇṇey-um*	orū thū*n*dū rottiyūm ve*nn*eyūm
Will you take some cake?	*koñjam paṇiyāram çāppiḍuvīrā?*	ko*ng*jūm pu*n*iyahrūm shahppidūveerah?
A small piece	*oru çiṟu tuṇḍu*	orū shirrū thū*n*dū
Make more toast	*iṉṉam adiga roṭṭi çūḍ' ākku*	innūm u*th*igū rotti shood' ahkkū
This is excellent tea	*idu migavum nalla tē*	i*th*ū migūvūm nullū thay

Health. (*Çaukkiyam.*)

(See Vocabulary 11, page 24.)

English.	Tamil (romanized).	Pronunciation.
How are you?	*çugam eppaḍi?*	shūgūm eppudi?
I am very well	*migavum çugamāy irukkiṟēṉ*	migūvūm shūgumahy irūkkirrayn
— — ill	*eṉakku-c-cugam il-läi*	enūkkū-ch-chūgūm ill*ay*
— — not very well	*eṉakku migavum çugam illai*	enūkkū migūvūm shūgūm ill*ay*
I hope you will soon be better	*çīkkiramāy çugam aḍāivīr eṉṟu nambugiṟēṉ*	sheekkirumahy shūgūm ūd*ay*veer endrū numbūgghirrayn
Do you sleep well?	*naṉṟāy-t-tūṅgugiṟīrā?*	nundrahy-th-thoongū-ghirreerah?
Pretty well, thank you	*koñjam naṉṟāy, umakku vandaṉam*	ko*ng*jūm nundrahy, ūmūkkū vun*th*ūnūm
I have caught a chill	*eṉakku kuḷir piḍitt' irukkiṟadu*	enūkkū kū*l*ir pidithth' irūkkirrū*th*ū
I feel sick	*viyādiyāy uṇarugiṟēṉ*	viyah*th*iyahy ūnūrūghirrayn

English.	Tamil (romanized).	Pronunciation.
Send for a doctor	*vaittiyaṉukku āḷ aṉuppu*	viththiyunūkkū ahl unūppū
I want to see a ...	*... pārkka vēṇḍum*	... pahrkkū vayndūm
She has a cough	*avaḷukku irumal piḍittukkoṇḍadu*	avulūkkū irūmūl pidiththūkkondūthū
Where is there a chemist's shop?	*raçāyaṉakkāraṉuḍäiya kaḍäi eṅgē-y-irukkiṟadu?*	rushahyūnūkkahrūnūdayyū kuday enggay-y-irūkkirrūthū?
How much is the doctor's fee for a visit?	*vaittiyaṉuḍäiya oru varugäikku çambaḷam eṉṉa?*	viththiyūnūdayyū orū vurūgaykkū shumbūlūm ennū?
Have this prescription made up	*inda vāgaḍamuṟäiyiṉ paḍi marundu koṇḍu vā*	inthū vahgūdūmūrrayyin pudi murūnthū kondū vah
One tablespoonful three times a day	*oru nāḷäikku mūṉṟu muṟäi oru mēçäik-k-karaṇḍi niṟäiya*	orū nahlaykkū moondrū mūrray orū mayshayk-kurūndi nirrayyū
To be taken after each meal	*ovvoru çāppāṭṭiṉ piṉ uṭkoḷḷa vēṇḍum*	ovvorū shahppahttin pin utkollū vayndūm
Shake the bottle	*pōttaläik-kulukku*	pohththulayk-kūlūkkū
Outward application only	*veḷippūççu māttiram*	velippoochchū mahththirūm
Poison	*viçam*	vishūm

The Time. (*Nēram.*)

(See Vocabulary 7, page 19.)

English	Tamil (romanized)	Pronunciation
Please tell me the time	*eṉakku nēram çolla tayavu çeyyum*	enūkkū nayrūm shollū thuyūvū sheyyūm
What time is it?	*maṇi nēram eṉṉa?*	muni nayrūm ennū?
Ten minutes past seven	*ēḻu maṇi pattu nimiçam çeṉṟadu*	eryū muni puththū nimishūm shendrūthū
It has just struck nine	*ippō oṉbadu maṇi aḍittadu*	ippoh onbūthū muni udiththūthū
The clock is striking...	*... maṇi-y-aḍikkiṟadu*	...muni-y-udikkirrūthū
A quarter past one	*oṉṟē kāl maṇi*	ondray kahl muni
It is past one	*oṉṟ' āyiṭṭu*	ondr'ahyittū
Half-past four	*nālaräi maṇi*	nahluray muni
Twenty minutes to six	*āṟu maṇikku irubadu nimiçam*	ahrrū munikku irūbūthū nimishūm
A quarter to eight	*eṭṭukku kāl maṇi irukkiṟadu*	ettūkkū kahl muni irūkkirrūthū

English.	Tamil (romanized).	Pronunciation.
By my watch	*en gadiyārappadi*	en gudiyahrū-p-pudi
Exactly 3 o'clock	*çariyāy mūnru mani*	shuriyahy moondrū muni
At what time?	*enda nērattil?*	enthū nayrūththil?
9.0 a.m.	*mut-pagal onbadu manikku* [*ku*	mūt-pugūl onbūthū munikkū
7.0 p.m.	*pit-pagal ēru manik-*	pit-pugūl ayryū munikkū
It is not late	*nēran çella-v-illäi* (or *çenrad' illäi*)	nayrūng shellū-v-illay (shendrūth' illay)
It is early	*nēram mundi-y-irukkiradu*	nayrūm mūnthi-y-irūk-kirrūthū

Post-office and Telegrams. (*Tapālāi-k-kurittu.*)

(See Vocabulary 20, page 39. For Postal Rates, see page 96.)

English.	Tamil (romanized).	Pronunciation.
Where is the telegraph (*or* post-) office?	*min tapāl çāvadi engē-y-irukkiradu?*	min thupahl shahvūdi enggay-y-irūkkirrūthū?
Have you any letters (telegrams, newspapers) for Mr. ...)	*kāgidam (tandi, çamāçārapattirigäi) edēnūm...turäikku irukkiradā?*	kahghithūm (thunthi, shumahshahrūpaththi-rigay ethaynūm...thū-raykkū irūkkirrūthah?
Will this letter go to-night?	*inda-k-kāgidam irāttirikku pōgumā?* [*rumbugirēn*	inthū-k-kahghithūm irahththirikkū poh-gūmah? [ghirrayn
I wish to send ...	...*kku anuppa vi-*	...kkū unūppū virūmbū-
What is the postage of this letter?	*inda-k-kāgidattukku tavāt çelavu enna?*	inthū-k-kahghithūththūk-kū thuvaht shelūvū ennū
To register a letter	*kāgidam padivu çeyya (tākkal panna)*	kahghithūm pudivū shey-yū (thahkkūl punnū)
What is the charge?	*çelavu enna?*	shelūvū ennū?
For the first ten words	*mudal pattu-c-cotkalukku*	mūthūl puththū-ch-chot-kūlūkkū
For every additional word	*idil adiga-c-cotkal ovvonrukku*	ithil uthigū-ch-chotkūl ovvondrūkkū
Name and address of sender	*anuppuvanudäiya peyar-um vakkanäi-y-um (vilāçam-um)*	unūppūvūnūdayyū pey-ūr-ūm vukkūnayyūm (vilahshūm-ūm)
Reply paid	*piratiyuttara-çelavu koduttu*	pirūthi-y-ūththūrū-shel-ūvū kodūththū
When is the next delivery?	*adutta tapāl-oppadäi eppō?*	udūththū thupahl-oppū-day eppoh?

English.	Tamil (romanized.)	Pronunciation.
When does the post-office close?	*tapāl çāvaḍi epporudu mūḍugiṟadu?*	thupahl shahvŭdi eppo-ryŭ*th*ū moodūghirrŭ*th*ū?
I want a money order for...	*...-kku maṉi ādar vēṇḍum*	...kkū muni ahdŭr vay*n*-dūm
Payable at...	*...-il koḍukkum paḍi*	...il kodŭkkūm pudi
Is the English mail in yet?	*ingilish tapāl iṉṉum irukkiṟadā?*	ingghilish thupahl in-nūm irūkkirrū*th*ah?
The latest delivery is at...	*kaḍäiçiyāṉa tapāl-oppaḍäi ...kku*	kud*ay*shiyahnŭ thupahl-oppŭd*ay* ...kkū

In Town. (*Nagarattil.*)

(See Vocabularies 8 & 18, pages 21 & 34.)

Where shall we go?	*eṅgē pōvōm?*	enggay pohvohm?
Let us go	*pōvōm (nām pōgaṭ-ṭum)*	pohvohm (nahm pohgut-tūm)
Which is the way to...?	*...ku vaṟi yedu?*	...kū vuryi ye*th*ū?
Where does this road lead to?	*inda vaṟi eṅgē po-giṟadu?*	in*th*ŭ vuryi enggay poh-ghirrŭ*th*ū?
Go up the street	*vītikku mēl pō*	veethikkū mayl poh
Is it far from here?	*adu ing' irundu dūramā?*	u*th*ū inggh' irūn*th*ū *th*oo-rŭmah?
How far is it to...?	*...kkū evvaḷavu dūram?*	...kkū evvu*l*ŭvū *th*oorŭm
Show me the way	*vaṟi kāṭṭu*	vuryi kahttū
Turn to the right	*valappakkam tirumbu*	vulŭppukkŭm thirūmbū
Go quickly	*çuṟukkāy-p-pō*	shūrrūkkahy-p-poh
— slowly	*mella mella pō*	mellŭ mellŭ poh
— straight on	*nērāy-p-pō*	nayrahy-p-poh
Keep to the left	*iḍa-p-pakkamāy-p-pō*	idu-p-pukkŭmahy-p-poh
Second turning to the right	*valappakkattil iraṇ-ḍām kuṟukku-vaṟi*	vulŭppukkŭththil iru*n*-dahm kūrrūkkū-vuryi
Take the first to the left and the second to the right	*iḍappakkattil mudal kuṟukku-vaṟi eḍut-tu valappakkattil iraṇḍām kuṟukku-vaṟiyāy tirumbi pō*	iduppukkŭththil mū*th*ŭl kūrrūkkū-vuryi eduth-thū vulŭppukkŭththil iru*n*dahm kūrrūkkū-vuryiyahy thirūmbi poh
Cross the road	*vīti kuṟukkē pō*	veethi kūrrūkkay poh
In what street is...?	*...enda vītiyil iruk-kiṟadu?*	...en*th*ŭ veethiyil irūk-kirrŭ*th*ū?
Please direct me the nearest way to...	*...kku kiṭṭiya vaṟi eṉṉäi-k-kaṭṭuṅgaḷ*	...kkū kittiyŭ vuryi en-*n*ayk-kahttūnggŭ*l*

English.	Tamil (romanized).	Pronunciation.
Is this the way to...? [F.?	*...kku vaṛi-y-idu tā-nā?* [*rīrā?*	...kkū vuryi-y-ithū thah-nah? [rah?
Do you know Mr.	*F. turäiyäi aṛigi-*	F. thūrayyay urrighiree-
I don't know any-one of that name [well	*anda-p-peyar koṇḍa evaräiyum nāṉ aṛi-yēṉ* [*t-teriyum*	unthū-p-peyūr kondū evarayyūm nahn urri-yayn [theriyūm
I know him very	*avar eṉakku nallāy-*	uvūr enūkkū nullahy-th-
Who is he?	*avar yār?*	uvūr yahr?
He is an old friend of mine	*avar eṉakku-p-paṛäiya çiṉēgidaṉ*	uvūr enūkkū-p-puryayyū shin-ayghithūn
Where does he live?	*avar eṅgē kuḍi-y-irukkiṛār?*	uvūr enggay kūdiyirūk-kirrahr?
Close by (me)	(*eṉakku-k-*) *kiṭṭa*	(enūkkū-k-) kittū
Can you take me to a good hotel?	*nalla viḍudikku eṉṉäi-k-kūṭṭi-k-koṇḍu pōvīrā?*	nullū vidūthikkū ennay-k-kootti-k-kondū poh-veerah?
Is Mr. F. (Mrs. F.) at home?	*F. turäi (turäi-çāṉi) avargaḷ vīṭṭil irukkiṛārā?*	F. thūray (thūrayshahni) uvūrgūl veettil irūk-kirrrahrah?
Good morning	*kālāi vandaṉam*	kahlay vunthūnūm
How do you do?	*çugam eppaḍi?*	shūgūm eppudi?
Very well	*metta naṉṟāy irukkiṛadu*	meththū nundrahy irūk-kirrūthū
I am very well	*nāṉ migavum çuga-māy irukkiṛēṉ*	nahn migūvūm shūgū-mahy irūkkirrayn
I must go	*nāṉ pōga vēṇḍum*	nahn pohgū vayndūm
Good-bye, farewell	*vandanam, pōyiṭṭu varuvēṉ*	vunthūnūm, pohyittū vurūvayn
I wish you good morning	*umakku kālāi van-daṉam tarugiṛēṉ*	ūmūkkū kahlay vunthū-nūm thurūghirrayn
Good evening	*çāyaṅkāla* } *vanda-*	shahyūngkahlū } vunthū-
Good night	*irāttiri* } *ṉam*	irahththiri } nūm
What is the name of that village?	*anda ūrukku peyar eṉṉa?*	unthū oorūkkū peyūr ennū?
What sort of a road is it?	*adu eṉṉa vagäiyāṉa vaṛi?*	uthū ennū vugayyahnū vuryi?
Which way am I to go?	*nāṉ enda vaṛiyāy-p-pōga vēṇḍum?*	nahn enthū vuryiyahy-p-pohgū vayndūm?
You are in the right way	*nīr çariyāṉa vaṛi-yil pōgiṛīr*	neer shuriyahnū vuryiyil pohghireer

English.	Tamil (romanised).	Pronunciation.
You are quite out of the way	*nīr muttum vaṛi tappi-p-pōgiṛīr*	neer mŭttŭm vuryi thup-pi-p-pohghirreer
Have you a card?	*uṉṉidam uṉ peyar-çīṭṭ' irukkiṛadā?*	ŭnnidŭm ŭn peyŭr-sheett' irŭkkirrŭthah?
Give him my card	*avarukku eṉ peyar-çīṭṭäik-koḍu*	uvŭrŭkkŭ en peyŭr-sheettay-k-kodŭ
I will call again	*maṟupaḍiyum pōyk-kāṇbēṉ*	murrŭpudiyŭm pohyk-kahnbayn
Does he expect you?	*avar uṉṉäi-k-kātt' irukkiṛārā?*	uvŭr ŭnnay-k-kahthth' irŭkkirrahrah?
He is expecting you	*avar uṉṉäi-k-kātt' irukkiṛār*	uvŭr ŭnnay-k-kahthth' irŭkkirrahr
I have an engagement with him	*avarōḍu eṉakku ōr aluval uṇḍu*	uvŭrohdŭ enŭkkŭ ohr ulŭvŭl ŭndŭ

Shopping. (*Koḷvaṉäi.*)

(See Vocabularies 4—6, 12—17, pages 15—19, 26—34. For Weights & Measures, see page 96.)

How much?	*evvaḷavu?*	evvŭlŭvŭ?
That is too much	*adu migavum adigam*	uthŭ migŭvŭm uthigŭm
What is the price?	*viläi eṉṉa?*	vilay ennŭ?
Will you send them at once?	*aväigaḷäi udaṉē aṉuppuvīrā?*	uvaygulay ŭdŭnay unŭp-pŭveerah?
I wish to buy...	*...vāṅga virumbu-giṟēṉ*	... vahnggŭ virŭmbŭ-ghirrayn
I will take this	*idäi eduppēṉ*	ithay edŭppayn
Send them to...	*aväigaḷäi...kku aṉuppu*	uvaygŭlay...kkŭ unŭppŭ
I want some calico	*eṉakku kālikkōpuḍa-väi koñjam vēṇum*	enŭkkŭ kahlikkoh pŭdŭ-vay kongjŭm vaynŭm
I should like to see some ribbons	*çila nāḍā-p-pārkka vēṇum*	shilŭ nahdah-p-pahrkkŭ vaynŭm
This colour is too dark—light	*inda niṟam metta iruṇḍadu—veḷiṟi-ṉadu*	inthŭ nirrŭm meththŭ irŭndŭthŭ — velirrinŭ-thŭ
Have you any narrower?—broader	*ummidam oḍuṅgi-yadu irukkiṟadā?—agalamāṉadu irukkiṟadā*	ŭmmidŭm odŭnghiyŭ-thŭ irŭkkirrŭthah?—ugŭlŭmahnŭthŭ iruk-kirrŭthah
What is this a yard?	*idu eṉṉa, oru ga-jamā (oru yārā)?*	ithŭ ennŭ, orŭ gujŭmah (orŭ yahrah)?

English.	Tamil (romanised).	Pronunciation.
It is faded	*adil niṟaṅ keṭṭadu*	u*th*il nirrung kettŭ*th*ū
Not so fine	*appaḍi nēttiyāṉadu vēṇḍām*	uppudi nayththiyahnŭ-*th*ū vay*n*dahm
This will do	*idu pōḍum*	i*th*ū poh*th*ūm
A skein of sewing silk	*taikkiṟa paṭṭu-nūṭ-pandu oṉṟu*	thikkirrŭ puttū-noo*t*-pun*th*ū ondrū
What are they a pair?	*aväigaḷ eṉṉa, oru jōḍiyā?*	uv*ay*gu*l* ennŭ, orū joh-diyah?
It is too dear	*adu metta kirākki*	u*th*ū meththū kirahkki
Try on these	*iväigaḷäi-y-iṭṭu-p-pār*	iv*ay*gŭ*lay*-y-ittū-p-pahr
They fit you very well	*aväigaḷumakkumiga naṉṟāy-p-porundum*	uv*ay*gŭ*l* ūmŭkkū migŭ nundrahy-p-porŭn*th*ūm
I will take them with me	*nāṉ aväigaḷäi-k-koṇḍu pōvēṉ*	nahn uv*ay*gŭ*lay*-k-kondŭ pohvayn
Make out my bill	*eṉ kaṇakku-k-koḍu*	en kunŭkkū-k-kodū

Shooting. (*Çikāri.*)

(See Vocabulary 21, page 10.)

English.	Tamil (romanised).	Pronunciation.
Have I to obtain permission to shoot here?	*iṅgē veḍiccuḍa nāṉ uttaravu peṟa vēṇḍumā?*	inggay vedichchūdū nahn ūththŭrŭvū perrū vay*n*-dūmah?
To whom must I apply?	*ārukku nāṉ pirāt-tippuc-ceyya vēṇḍum?*	ahrūkkū nahn pirahth-thipūch-cheyyŭ vay*n*-dūm?
What kind of game can I get here?	*nāṉ ivvidattil eṉṉa vēṭṭäi-y-āḍa-k-kūḍum?*	nahn ivvidŭththil ennŭ vaytt*ay*-y-ahdŭ-k-koodūm?
Elk, deer, hare, wild buffalo, boar, fox, tiger, elephant, &c.	*marāi, mān, muyal, kāṭṭ'erumäi, kāṭṭu-p-paṉṟi, nari, puli, yāṉäi mudalāṉaväi*	mur*ay*, mahn, mūyŭl, kahtterūm*ay*, kahttū-p-pundri, nuri, pūli, yahn*ay* mū*th*ūlahnŭv*ay*
Can I obtain the exclusive right over the shooting?	*nāṉ veḍi-c-cuḍuda-lukku-p-puṟa-niṅgalāṉa urimäi peṭṭu-k-koḷḷa-k-kūḍumā?*	nahn vedich-chūdū*th*ū-lūkkū-p-pūrū-neenggū-lahnū ūrim*ay* pe*tt*ū-k-ko*ll*ū-k-koodūmah?
What rent must I pay?	*nāṉ eṉṉa vari* (or *vāḍagäi*) *koḍukka vēṇum?*	nahn ennŭ vuri (vahdū-*gay*) kodūkku vay*n*ūm?

English.	Tamil (romanized).	Pronunciation.
Can I get one or two experienced men to go out shooting with me?	*eṉṉōḍu kūḍa veḍi-c-cuḍa-p-pōga oṉṟu alladu iraṇḍu paṟakkamāṉa ālgaḷ kiḍäikka-k-kūḍumā?*	ennohdŭ koodŭ vedich-chŭdŭ-p-pohgŭ ondrŭ ullŭ*th*ŭ irundŭ puryŭkkŭmahnŭ ah*l*gŭ*l* kidaykkŭ-k-koodŭmah?
How much must I pay each of them per day (week)?	*avargaḷ-ovvoruvarukkum, nāḷ oṉṟiṭku (vāram oṉṟiṭku) evvaḷavu koḍukka vēṇḍum?*	uvŭrgŭ*l* ovvorŭvŭrŭkkŭm, nah*l* ondri*tk*ŭ (vahrŭm ondri*tk*ŭ) evvu*l*ŭvŭ kodŭkkŭ vay*n*dŭm?
How many dogs will you let me have?	*ettaṉäi nāy eṉakku-k-koḍuppīrā?*	eththun*ay* nahy enŭkkŭ-k-kodŭppeerah?
Are the dogs properly trained?	*anda nāygaḷ çariyāy-p-paṟakkap-paṭṭaväigaḷā?*	un*th*ŭ nahygŭ*l* shuriyahy-p-puryŭkkŭp-p-puttŭv*ay*gŭ*l*ah?
Keep the dogs back	*nāygaḷäi-p-piṉṉē vaittu-k-koḷ*	nahygu*lay*-p-pinnay v*i*ththŭkko*l*
Load my gun	*eṉ tuppākkikku marundu pōḍu*	en thŭppahkkikkŭ murŭn*th*ŭ pohdŭ
Carry my gun	*eṉ tuppākkiyäi-y-eḍuttu-k-koṇḍu pō*	en thŭppahkkiy*ay*-y-edŭththŭ-k-ko*n*dŭ poh
Give me some cartridges	*eṉakku çila tōṭṭā-k-koḍu*	enŭkkŭ shilŭ thohttah-k-kodŭ
Do not fire!	*çuḍādē!*	shŭdah*th*ay
Let me have a shot with your gun	*umadu tuppākkiyāl nāṉ oru çūḍu çuḍaṭṭum*	ŭmŭ*th*ŭ thŭppahkkiyahl nahn orŭ shoodŭ shŭduttŭm
To cock a gun	*tuppākkik-kudiräiyäi iṛuttu viḍa*	thŭppahkkikkŭ*th*ir*ayyay* iryŭththŭ vidŭ

Fishing. (*Mīṉ-vēṭṭäi.*)

(See Vocabulary 21, page 40.)

English.	Tamil (romanized).	Pronunciation.
Is there any fishing to be had near here?	*ivviḍattukku-k-kiṭṭa mīṉ piḍikka-k-kūḍumā?*	ivvidŭththŭkkŭ-k-kittŭ meen pidikkŭ-k-koodŭmah?
Must I first obtain permission to fish?	*mīṉ piḍikka nāṉ mudal uttaravu peṟa vēṇḍumā?*	meen pidikkŭ nahn mŭ*th*ŭl ŭththŭrŭvŭ perrŭ vay*n*dŭmah?
What is the rent for fishing in this river (lake) (pond)?	*inda āṟṟil (ēriyil) (kuḷattil) mīṉ piḍikka vari-y-eṉṉa?*	in*th*ŭ ah*tt*il (ayriyil) (kŭ*l*ŭththil) meen pidikkŭ vuri-y-ennŭ?

English.	Tamil (romanized).	Pronunciation.
Can I get the sole right of fishing?	*mīṉ piḍikkiṟadaṯku nāṉ taṉi urimäi peṟa-k-kūḍumā?*	meen pidikkirrŭ*th*ŭ*t*kū nahn thuni ūrim*ay* perrŭ-k-koodūmah ?
Can I have a boat and man?	*eṉakku oru vaḷḷam-um* (or *dōṉiyum*) *āḷ-um kiḍäikkumā?*	enŭkkū orū vu*ll*ŭm-ūm (*th*ohniyūm) ah*l*ūm kid*ay*kkūmah ?
What do you charge for the hour (day)?	*oru maṇikku* (*nāḷukku*) *evvaḷavu kūli kēṭkiṟāy?*	orū mu*n*ikkū (nah*l*ŭkkū) evvu*l*ŭvŭ koo*l*i kaytkirrahy ?
Are you an experienced fisherman?	*nī parākkamāṉa mīṉ-piḍi-kāraṉa?*	nee puryukkūmahnŭ meen-pidi-kahrūnah ?
Can I depend on you?	*nāṉ uṉṉil nambikkäi vaikka-k-kūḍumā?*	nahn unnil numbikk*ay* vikkŭkkoodūmah ?
The oar	*taṇḍu: tuḍuppu*	thundū ; thūdūppū
Have you brought some bait?	*koñjam iräi koṇḍu vand' irukkiṟāyā?*	kon*g*jūm ir*ay* ko*n*dū vun*th*'irūkkirrahyah ?
What bait must I use?	*eṉṉa iräi upayōgikka vēṇḍum?*	ennŭ ir*ay* ūpūyohghikkū vay*n*dūm ?
Will you bring bait?	*iräi koṇḍu varuvāyā?*	ir*ay* ko*n*dū vurūvahyah ?
Give me a hook	*oru tūṇḍil koḍu*	orū thoo*n*dil kodū
Will you bait my line?	*eṉ tūṇḍilukku iräi pōḍuvāyā?*	en thoo*n*dilūkkū ir*ay* pohdūvahyah ?
Give me my rod	*eṉ kōläi eṉakku-k-koḍu*	en kohl*ay* enŭkkū-k-kodū
Row gently	*meduvāy taṇḍu vali* (or *çavaḷ vali*)	me*th*ūvahy thu*n*dū vuli (shuvŭl vuli)
Do not make a noise	*çandaḍi paṇṇādē*	shun*th*udi pu*nn*ah*th*ay
Make haste!	*çīkkiram paṇṇu!*	sheekkirūm pu*nn*ū !
The fishing is good here	*mīṉ-piḍippu ivvidattil nalladu*	meen-pidippū ivvidŭththil nullŭ*th*ū
How much does this fish weigh?	*inda mīṉ evvaḷavu niṟukkiṟadu?*	in*th*ŭ meen evvu*l*ŭvŭ nirrūkkirrŭ*th*ū ?
Will you weigh it?	*adäi niṟuppāyā?*	u*th*ay nirrūppahyah ?

Commercial and Trading. (*Viyāpāram.*)

(See Vocabulary 10, page 35.)

English.	Tamil (romanized).	Pronunciation.
Send in my account	*eṉ kaṇakkäi aṉuppu*	en ku*n*ŭkk*ay* unūppū
I am leaving to-morrow	*nāṉ nāḷäikku-p-pōgiṟēṉ*	nahn nah*lay*kkū-p-pohghirrayn
You have over-charged me	*nī adiga viläi pōṭṭ' irukkiṟāy*	nee u*th*igŭ vil*ay* pohtt' irūkkirrahy

English.	Tamil (romanized).	Pronunciation.
Give me a receipt	*paṯṯuc-cīṭṭu eṉakku-k-koḍu*	puttūch-cheettū yenūkkū-k-kodū
The firm has failed	*inda varttagar kūṭṭam muṟindu pōy-irukkiṟadu*	inthū vurththūgūr koot-tūm murrinthū pohy-irūkkirrūthū
What are the assets?	*kaḍaṉ irukka-p-pōdumāṉa poruḷ evvaḷavu?*	kudūn irrūkkū-p-pohthū-mahnu porūl evvulūvū?
Show me a balance-sheet	*pākkittāḷ eṉakku-k-kāṭṭu*	bahkkiththahl enūkkū-k-kahttū
What are the liabilities?	*kaḍaṉ* (or *uttaravādam*) *evvaḷavu?*	kudūn (uththūrūvahthūm) evvulūvū?
There is an error in your account	*uṉ kaṇakkil oru tappidam irukkiṟadu*	ūn kunūkkil orū thuppithūm irūkkirrūthū
My samples are delayed	*eṉadu mādiri-çāmāṉgaḷ tāmadap-paṭṭ' irukkiṉṟaṉa*	enūthū mahthiri-shah-mahngūl thahmūthūp-putt' irūkkindrūnū
I want to get them through the Custom House	*tīrvāi-vīṭṭu-vaṟiyāga nāṉ avāigaḷāi adāiya vēṇḍum*	theervay-veettu-vuryi-yahgū nahn uvaygūlay udayyū vayndūm
I want a detailed statement	*eṉakku oru vivarac-cīṭṭu vēṇum*	enūkkū orū vivūrū-ch-cheettū vaynūm
I shall send in a claim	*nāṉ oru toḍarcci paṇṇuvēṉ*	nahn orū thodūrchchi punnūvayn
Can I insure my luggage?	*eṉ payaṇa-c-cāmāṉgaḷ uttaravādam paṇṇa-k-kūḍumā?*	en puyūnū-ch-chahmahn-gūl ūththūrūvahthūm punnū-k-koodūmah?
What is the rate?	*vīdam eṉṉa?*	veethūm ennū?
What is the charge?	*vilāi* (or *çelavu*) *eṉṉa*	vilay (shelūvu) ennū?
Will you accept a bill?	*oru uṇḍiyal ēṭṭu-k-koḷḷuvīrā?*	oru ūndiyūl ayttūk-kol-lūveerah
At three months	*mūṉṟu mādattil*	moondrū mahthūththil
Send by fast train	*kaḍi vaṇḍit-toḍar mūlamāga aṉuppu*	kuthi vundith-thodūr moolūmahgū unūppū
They can go by goods train	*avāigaḷ çāmāṉ-vaṇḍit-toḍar mūlam-āga pōgum*	uvaygūl shahmahn-vun-dith-thodūr moolūmah-gū pohgūm
What dividend is declared?	*eṉṉa pāgam aṟivikka-p-paḍugiṟadu?*	ennū pahgūm urrivik-kūp-pudūghirrathū?
Your luggage is liable to duty	*uṉ payaṇa-c-cāmāṉ tīrvāikku ēduvāy irukkiṟadu*	ūn puyūnū-ch-chahmahn theervaykkū aythūvahy irūkkirrūthū

English.	Tamil (romanized).	Pronunciation.
This cheque needs endorsing	*inda-c-cekkukku mēl oppam vēṇum*	in*th*ū-ch-chekkūkkū mayl oppūm vay*n*ūm
Have you declared the value?	*peṟumadi* (or *vilāi*) *çolli-y-irukkiṟīrā?*	perrūmŭ*thi* (vil*ay*) sholli-y-irūkkirreerah
I will prepay the carriage	*ēṯṯukkūli muṉ çeluttuvēṉ*	a*yt*tukkooli mūn sheluth-thūvayn
I have a letter of introduction	*utpaḍuttum kāgidam eṉakku uṇḍu*	ūtpudūththūm kahghi*th*ūm enūkkū ū*n*dū
Give me your estimate	*uṉ madippāi eṉakku-k-koḍu*	ūn mu*th*ipp*ay* enūkkū-k-kodū
Quote me a price	*oru vilāi eṉakku-c-collu*	oru vil*ay* enūkkūch-cholli
Public Works. (*Kaṭṭu-vēlāi.*)		
Come here with your hoe	*uṉ maṉveṭṭiyōḍu iṅgē vā*	ūn mu*n*vettiyohdū ing-gay vah
Bring (it) here	*iṅgē koṇḍu vā*	ing-gay ko*n*dū vah
Don't dig there	*aṅgē tōṇḍa vēṇḍām*	ung-gay thoh*n*dū vay*n*-dahm
Dig wider	*iṉṉam agalamāy veṭṭu*	innūm ugūlūmahy vettū
How many men are wanted to cut the jungle?	*kāḍu veṭṭa ettaṉāi āḷ tēvāi?*	kahdū vettū (y)eththū-*nay* ah*l* thayv*ay*?
Six men are wanted for road work	*rōttu vēlāikku āṟu āḷ vēṇḍum*	rohttū vayl*ay*kkū ahrrū ah*l* vay*n*dūm
Send three men to help the carpenters	*taccargaḷukku udavi çeyya mūṉṟu pērāi aṉuppu*	thuchchūrgū*l*ūkkū ū*th*ū-vi sheyyū moondrū pay-r*ay* unūppū
Take six men to build the bridge	*pālaṅ kaṭṭugiṟadaṯku āṟu pērāi eḍu*	pahlūng kuttūghirrū*th*ūt-kū ahrrū payr*ay* (y)edū
What kind of soil is there at that place?	*anda iḍattil eṉṉa vidamāṉa maṇṇu irukkiṟadu?*	un*th*ū idūththil ennū vi-*th*ūmahnū mu*n*nū irūk-kirrū*th*ū?
Very sandy	*migavum maṇal nilam*	migūvūm mu*n*ūl nilūm
Where was this stiff clay got?	*inda-t-taḍippāṉa maṇ eṅgē kiḍāittadu?*	in*th*ū-th-thudippahnū mu*n* engg*ay* kid*ay*th-thū*th*ū?
This is exceedingly hard ground	*idu mettavum kaḍuṉ tarāi*	i*th*ū meththūvūm kudūn thur*ay*
The hoe will break	*maṉveṭṭi uḍāiyum*	mu*n*vetti ūd*ay*yūm
A pickaxe will be required here	*iṅgē oru kōḍāli vēṇḍiyadu*	inggay orū kohdahli vay*n*diyū*th*ū

English.	Tamil (romanized).	Pronunciation.
Remove the stones with a crowbar [yungal	*kattappārāikkondu kallugalāi eduttu-p-pōdu*	kuttūppahraykkondū kullūgūlay edūththū-p-pohdū [gūl
Blast out the rock	*pārāikku vedi vai-*	pahrraykkū vedi viyūng-
Put aside all stones suitable for the foundation	*astivārattukku udavum katkalāi ellām oru pakkattil pōdu*	usthivahrūththūkkū ūthūvūm kutkūlay ellahm orū pukkūththil pohdū
The space is not [sufficient	*idam pōdādu*	idūm pohthahthū
Measure a foot and a half	*onrarāi adi ala*	ondr'uray udi ulū
Level thirty feet further back	*innam pinnukku muppadu adi çamam ākku*	innūm pinnūkkū mūppūthū udi shumūm ahkkū
The ground is very soft; you must therefore lay down a plank	*nilam metta çaduppu; āgāiyāl nī oru palagāi pōda vēndum*	nilūm meththū shuthūppū; ahgayyahl nee orū pulūgay pohdū vayndūm
Come this way; this ground is harder	*inda variyāy vā; indanilam metta kadumāiyāy irukkiradu*	inthū vuryiyahy vah; inthū nilūm meththū kudūmayyahy irūkkirrūthū
Bring the line and pegs to mark out the foundation	*astivārattāi-k-kurikkum padi kayir'-um mulāi-y-um kondu vārungal*	usthivahrūththay-k-kūrrikkūm pudi kuyirrūm mūlayyūm kondū vahrūnggūl
Must this work be done to-day?	*inda vēlāi inrāikku çeyya vēndumā?*	inthū vaylay indraykkūsheyyū vayndūmah?
How do you arrange the bricks in this kiln?	*nīngal inda-c-cūlāi-yil çengal eppadi adukkugirīrgal?*	neenggūl inthū-ch-choolayyil shenggul (y)eppūdi udūkkūghirreerggūl?
I want to build a house	*enakku oru vīttāik-katta vēndum*	(y)enūkkū orū veettaykkattū vayndūm
When will you bring me the estimate?	*madippu epporudu kondu varuvāy?*	muthippū (y)epporyūthū kondū vurūvahy?
Your estimate is too high	*un madippu-t-togāi adigam*	ūn muthippū-th-thogay uthigūm
I shall come frequently and see how the work is progressing	*vēlāi-y-eppadi nadand' ēri varugirād' enru adikkadi vandu pārppēn*	vaylay-yeppūdi nudūnth' ayrri vurūghirrūth' endrū udikkudi vunthū pahrppayn

English.	Tamil (romanized).	Pronunciation.
There is not enough sand in this mortar	*indaccunnāmbil maṇal pōdādu*	inthŭ-ch-chunnahmbil munŭl pohthahthŭ
The foundation must be compact and strong	*astivāram kettiyāy-um palamāy-um irukka vēṇḍum*	usthivahrŭm kettiyahy-ŭm bulŭmahyŭm irŭkka vayndŭm
You are wasting lime	*çuṇṇāmbäi vīṇāy-c-celavarikkiṟāy*	shŭnnahmbay veenahy-ch-chelavuryikkirrahy
Let the doors and windows be well fitted	*kadavugaḷum çaṉṉalgaḷum çariyāy porundi irukkaṭṭum*	kuthŭvŭgŭlŭm shunnŭlgŭlŭm shuriyahy porŭnthi irŭkk'uttŭm
The plastering of the wall must be done neatly	*çuvarukku nēttiyāy-c-cāndu pūçappaḍa vēṇḍum*	shŭvŭrŭkkŭ nayththiyahy-ch-chahnthŭ pooshŭppudŭ vayndŭm
White ants will attack the timber; tar it	*kaṟäiyāṉ marattil-ē piḍikkum; tāru pūçu*	kurrayyahn murŭththilay pidikkŭm; thahrŭ pooshŭ
These tiles are not good	*inda ōḍu nallad' alla*	inthŭ ohdŭ nullŭth' ullŭ
If a heavy shower of rain falls, many of the tiles will be destroyed	*periya maṟäi peydāl anēga ōḍu çēdamāy-p-pōgum* (or *pōm*)	periyŭ maryay peythahl unayggŭ ohdŭ shaythŭmahy-p-pohgŭm (pohm)
Thatch the roof	*kūräi mēy*	kooray mayy
Is the thatch ready?	*kūräikku-p-pul āyattamā?*	kooraykkŭ-p-pŭl ahyŭththŭmah?
Fasten it firmly	*adäi uṟudiyāy-k-kaṭṭu*	uthay ŭrrŭthiyahy-k-kuttŭ
Tar the floor	*taḷattukku-k-kīl pūçu*	thulŭththŭkkŭ-k-keel pooshŭ
Put cement over it	*adinmēl çimanti pūçu*	uthin-mayl shimunthi pooshŭ
Lay large stones across	*peruṅ kaṯkaḷäi kurukkē pōḍu*	perung kutkŭlay kŭrrŭkkay pohdŭ
Bring the chain	*çaṅgili koṇḍu vā*	shungghili kondŭ vah
Hold your pole in a line with the theodolite and the other pole	*uṉ kambäi tiyōḍalaiṭṭukkum maṭṭa-k-kambukk'um nērāga-p-piḍi*	ŭn kumbay thiyodŭlittŭkkŭm muttŭ-k-kumbŭkkŭm nayrahgŭ-p-pidi
Take the chain and iron pegs, and go there	*çaṅgiliyäi-y-um iruppu muḷäigaḷäi-y-um eḍuttu-k-koṇḍu aṅgē pō*	shungghiliyayyŭm irŭppŭ mŭlaygŭlayyŭm edŭththŭ-k-kondŭ unggay poh
Where are the iron pegs?	*ir muḷäigaḷ eṅgē?*	irŭppŭ mŭlaygŭl enggay?

English.	Tamil (romanized).	Pronunciation.
You go in the direction of that flag, and put down pegs	*nī anda-k-koḍikku nērē pōy muḷäigaḷäi aḍi*	nee unthū-k-kodikkū nayray pohy mūlaygūlay udi

Planting. (*Tōṭṭavēläi.*)

English.	Tamil (romanized).	Pronunciation.
How many coolies have you?	*uṉakku ettaṉäi kūliyāḷ uṇḍu?*	ünūkkū eththūnay kooliyahl ündū?
How many of them are women and children?	*avargaḷil peṇgaḷ-um, piḷḷäigaḷ-um ettaṉäi?*	uvūrgūlil pengūlūm, pillaygūlūm eththūnay?
How long have they been with you?	*avārgaḷ evvaḷavu kālamāy uṉṉiḍattil irukkiṟārgaḷ?*	uvūrgūl evvulūvū kahlūmahy ünnidūththil irūkkirrahrgūl?
Are they good workers?	*avargaḷ nalla vēläikkārarā?*	uvūrgūl nullū vaylaykkahrūrah?
If you work for me, you must be diligent, orderly, and obedient	*eṉṉiḍattil vēläi çeyvāy āṉāl nī çuṟuçuṟuppāy-um, oruṅgāy-um, kīrppaṉivāy-um irukka vēṇḍum*	ennidūththil vaylay sheyvahy ahnahl nee shūrrūshūrrūppahyūm, oryūng-gahyūm, keeryppunivahyūm irūkkū vayndūm
Call in the coolies	*kūlikkārarāi-k-kūppiḍu*	koolikkahrūray-k-kooppidū
Muster them near the bungalow	*bangalā kiṭṭa tiraṭṭuvai*	bunggūlah kittū thirutti vi
On account of the rain you have done only half a day's work	*maṟäiyi'ṉimittam arāi nāḷ vēläi māttiram çeydīrgaḷ*	muryayyi'nimiththūm uray nahl vaylay mahththirūm sheytheergūl
I did not see you in the working place	*uṉṉäi vēläi-t-talattilē kāṇa-v-illäi*	ūnnay vaylayth-thulūththilay kahnū-v-illay
Take all the tools	*ellā āyūdaṅgaḷäiyum eḍuṅgaḷ*	ellah ahyūthūnggūlayyūm edūnggūl
Go to the hill	*maläikku-p-pōṅgaḷ*	mulaykkū-p-pohnggūl
Each man must dig forty holes a day	*ovvōr āḷ nāṭpadu kuṛi oru nāḷäiyil veṭṭa vēṇḍum*	ovvohr ahl nahtpūthū kūryi orū nahlayyil vettū vayndūm
Do not pull up the plants	*nāṯṯugaḷäi-p-piḍuṅgādē*	nahttūgūlay-p-pidūnggahthay
Mark the place where you must dig	*nī veṭṭa vēṇḍiya iḍattäi-k-kuṛi*	nee vettū vayndiyū idūththay-k-kūrri

English.	Tamil (romanized).	Pronunciation.
Trample the earth down	*maṇṇäi midittu-p-pōḍu*	munnay mithith-thūp-pohdū
The dug-out earth is useless; put in only new earth	*veṭṭiṉa maṉ udavādu; pudu maṉ māttiram pōḍu*	vettinū mun ūthūvahthū; pūthū mun mahththirūm pohdū
Go and fetch the plants from the nursery	*nāṯṯumēḍäikku-p-pōy kaṉṟu eduttu-k-koṇḍu vāruṅgaḷ*	nahttūmaydaykkū-p-pohy kundrū edūththū-k-kondū vahrūnggūl
Take up the plants with the earth	*kaṉṟugaḷäi maṇṇōḍu eḍu*	kundrūgūlay munnohdū edū

Changing Money. (*Paṇam-māṯṯu.*)

(For Tables of Money, see pages 95 and 96.)

Where can I get money changed?	*nāṉ eṅgē paṇam māṯṯa-k-kūḍum?*	nahn enggay punūm mahttū-k-koodūm?
Where is the bank (a money-changer)?	*vaṅgu-çālāi (paṇam māṯṯum iḍam) eṅgē-y-irukkiṟadu?*	vungū-shahlay (punūm mahttūm idum) enggay-y-irukkirrūthū?
I want change for a five-pound note	*eṉakku aindu pavuṇḍ nōṭṭukku māṯṯu vēṇum*	enūkkū inthū puvūnd nohttūkkū mahttū vaynūm
Will you give me Indian money?	*eṉakku indiyāp-paṇam koḍuppīrā?*	enūkkū inthiyahppunūm kodūppeerah?
What is the exchange on English money?	*iṅgilish paṇattil māṯṯum vaṭṭam eṉṉa?*	ingghilish punūththil mahttūm vuttūm ennu?
Will you change me a sovereign?	*eṉakku oru çavaräin māṯṯuvīrā?*	enūkkū orū suvūrayn mahttūveerah?
Will you cash this cheque for me?	*inda-c-cekkäi eṉakku kāç' ākkuvīrā?*	inthū-ch-chekkay enūkkū kahsh' ahkkūveerah?
Please give me gold and silver, not paper money	*poṉ, veḷḷi nāṇayamāy-k-koḍukkavum; kaḍudāçi paṇam vēṇḍām*	pon, velli nahnūyūmahy-k-kodūkkūvūm; kudūthahshi punūm vayndahm
A bill of exchange	*uṇḍiyal* (or *paṇam māṯṯum çīṭṭu*)	ūndiyūl (punūm mahttūm sheettū)
It is payable at sight	*kāṭṭiṉa pōdu māṯṯa vēṇḍiyadu*	kahttinū pohthū mahttū vayndiyūthū
Give me the amount in rupees	*eṉakku anda togäiyäi rūbāyil koḍu*	(y)enūkkū unthū thogayyay roobahyil kodū

ENGLISH-TAMIL VOCABULARY.*

Note.—1. This Vocabulary is intended to be merely supplementary to the classified lists of words in the first part of the book.

2. Only the base-forms of verbs are given. For their conjugation, the student must consult *Tamil Grammar Self-Taught* and the Tamil-English Dictionary.

3. If any English word cannot be found here, try the nearest synonym.

4. n. = noun; v. = verb; a. = adjective; adv. = adverb; prep. = preposition; tr. = transitive; intr. = intransitive.

A, an, *oru, ōr.*
abandon, *viṭṭuviḍu, kai-viḍu.*
able, *vallamäi-y-uḷḷa.* See also "can."
about, prep., *kuṟittu, kiṭṭa*
above, *mēl-ē.*
absent, a., *illāda; varāda.*
absurd, *paittiyamāṉa.*
abundance, *migudi, tiraḷ.*
abundantly, *tiraḷāga.*
abuse, n., *tūshaṇäi, ēçal.*
abuse, v., *vai, tiṭṭu, ēçu.*
accept, *ēṯṯukkoḷ.*
accident, *iḍäiyūṟu, vikkiṉam.*
accommodation, *vaçadi.*
accompany, *kūḍa-p-pō.*
according to, *paḍi.*
account, n., *kaṇakku.*
account-book, *kaṇakku-p-pustagam.*
accountant, *kaṇakkaṉ.*
accumulate, *kuvi, çēr, kūṭṭu.*
accuracy, *tiṭṭam.*
accuse, v., *kuṯṯañ-çāṭṭu.*
accused (person), *kuṯṯañ-çāṭṭappaṭṭavaṉ, edirāḷi.*
accustomed, *paḻagiṉa.*
accustomed (to be), *paḻagu.*

ache, n., *vali; nōvu.*
ache, v., *nō, vali, iḍi.*
acknowledge, *oṭṭukkoḷ.*
acquaintance, *aṟimugam.*
acre, *ēkkar.*
act, n., *çeygäi; kiriyäi.*
active, *çākkiradäiyāṉa.*
actually, in reality, *uḷḷapaḍi.*
acute, *kūrmäiyāṉa.*
address (on a letter), n., *mēl vilāçam.*
advance (money), n., *aççāram; muṭpaṇam.*
advance, v., *mundip-pō.*
advocate, n., *aṭṭuvakkāṭṭu, niyāya vādi;* v., *parindu pēçu.*
affair, *çaṅgadi, kāriyam.*
affection, *aṉbu, nēçam.*
after, *piṉbu, piṉṉālē.*
again, *maṟupaḍiyum tirumbavum.*
against, *virōdamāy.*
age (of a person or animal), *vayaçu, āyuçu.*
age (period), *kālam, yugam.*
aged, *vayadu çeṉṟa.*
ago, *muṉṉē.*
agree, *çammati, amäi.*
agreement (compact), *uḍaṉpaḍikkäi.*

* For Tamil-English Vocabulary, see *Tamil Grammar Self-Taught.*

agriculture, *vēḷāṇmäi.*
aid, n., *tuṇäi, ottāçäi.*
alarm, v., *payappaḍuttu, tigäi*; n., *tigäippu.*
alight, v., *iṟaṅgu.*
all, *ellām; ellārum.*
allow, *idaṅ koḍu.*
almost, *koñjaṅ kuṟäiya.*
alms, *piccäi, dāṉam*
alone, *taṉiyē.*
along, *neḍuga.*
along with, *kūḍa.*
aloud, *çattamāy, urakka.*
already, *muṉṉamē.*
also, *um; kūḍa.*
alter, *māṭṭu.*
alternately, *māṟi māṟi.*
always, *epporudum.*
amid, *naḍuvilē.*
among, *uḷ.*
amount, *togäi.*
an, *oru.*
and, *um.*
anew, *pudidāy.*
anger, *ericcal, kōbam.*
angry, *kōbamuḷḷa.*
annual, *varushāntara.*
another, *iṉṉoru.*
answer, n., *uttaravu; maṟu-* [*mori.*
anvil, *aḍäi-kal.*
any, a., *yādoru.*
apart, *vervēṟāy, pirivāy.*
appear, *tōṉṟu.*
appearance, *tōṭṭam, āçar.*
appetite, *paçi.*
appoint, *niyami.*
approach, v., *çēr, kiṭṭappō.*
arch, n., *vaḷäivu.*
arise, *eṟund'iru.*
around, *çuṭṭi; çūṟa.*
arrack, *çārāyam.*

arrive, *vandu-ç-çēr.*
as, *pōl; paḍi.*
ascend, *ēṟu.*
aside, *oru pakkattil.*
ask, *kēḷ.*
asleep, *nittiräiyāy.* [*çey.*
assist, *udavi-çey, udavu, tuṇäi-*
attempt, n., *pirayattaṉam.*
attend, *kūḍa-p-pō; kavaṉi.*
attention, *kavaṉam.*
auction, *ēlam.*
authority, *adigāram.*
awake, a., *viṟippāṉa.*
awake, to, (tr.) *eṟuppu;* (intr.)
away, *tūra.* [*viṟi, eṟund'iru.*

Baby, *kuṟandäi.*
back, adv., *piṉṉē; tirumba.*
bad (evil), *keṭṭa.*
bag, *pai.*
bait, n., *irāi.*
balance in hand, *kai-y-iruppu.*
ball (globe), *uṇḍäi, pandu.*
bamboo, *mūṅgil.*
band (of persons), *kūṭṭam.*
bandage, *kaṭṭu.*
bar (of a door), *tāṟppāḷ;* (obstacle) *taḍäi.*
bare, *niruvāṉa, veṟu.*
bark, n. (of tree), *paṭṭäi;* (of dog) *kuläittal;* v., *kuläi.*
barrenness, *pāṟ.*
base, n., (bottom) *aḍi;* a., *kīṟāṉa, nīça.*
battle, n., *pōr, yuddam.*
bazaar-man, *kaḍäikkāraṉ.*
be, *iru.*
bear (support, endure), *tāngu: çuma.*
beat, v., *aḍi.*
beauty, *aṟagu.*

because, *ēṉ-eṉṟāl*.
beckon, *çaigäi kāṭṭu*.
become, *āgu*.
before, *muṉ, muṉṉe*.
beg alms, *piççäi kēḷ*.
begin, *toḍangu, tuvakku*.
beginning, &c., *ādimudal*.
behind (time), *piṟagu*.
behind, *piṉṉē*.
behold! *idō pār*.
belief, *viçuvāçam*.
belong, *çēr, aḍu*.
belonging to, a., *aḍutta, uriya*.
below, *kīṟe; paṇiya*.
bend, v., *vaḷäi, kōṭṭu*.
besides, *arugē, pakkattil: tavira*.
best, *uttamam*.
betel, *veṯṯiläi*.
between, *naḍuvē, ūḍē*.
beyond, *appāl, appuṟattil*.
bid (a price), v., *viläi kēḷ*.
bid (order), v., *kaṭṭaḷäi-y-iḍu*.
big, *periya; parutta*.
bind, v., *kaṭṭu*.
bird, *kuruvi, paṭçi*.
birth, *piṟappu*.
birthday, *jaṉma-vāram*.
bite, n. & v., *kaḍi*.
bitter, *kaçanda; kaçappāṉa*.
blade (weapon), *alagu*.
blame, n., *kuṯṯam; v., kuṯṯañ-çāṭṭu*.
bleed, v. intr., *irattam vaḍi; tr., irattañ kuttivāṅgu*.
blessing, n., *āçīrvādam*.
block, n., *kaṭṭäi*.
blossom, n., *pū; malar; v., alar, pushpi*.
blow, v., *ūdu; n., aḍi, kuṭṭu*.
bluntness, *maṟuṅgal*.
boil, v., *kodi; avi; kāyççu*.
boil, n., *paru, kaṭṭi*
boiled rice, *çōṟu*.
bolt, n., *tārppāḷ; tirāṅgu*.
bond (of debt), *kaḍaṉçīṭṭu*.
book, *pustagam*.
borrow, *iraval* (or *kaḍaṉ*) *vāṅgu*.
bottle, *pōttal; puṭṭi*.
bottom, n., *aḍi; kīrppakkam*.
boundary, *elläi*.
bow (weapon), n., *vil*; v., *vaḷäi*; (salute) *vaṇaṅgu*.
box, n., *peṭṭi*.
bran, *taviḍu*.
branch, *kombu*.
brand, v., *kuṟiçuḍu; n., koḷḷi*.
breadth, *agalam*.
break, v., *muṟi; uḍäi*.
breath, *çuvāçam; mūççu*.
breathe, *çuvāçam-iḍu*.
breeze, *iḷaṅkāṯṯu*.
bribe, n., *kaikkūli*.
brick, *çeṅgal*.
bride, *maṇavāḷi*.
bridegroom, *māppiḷḷäi*.
bridesmaid, *tōṛi*.
bridge, *pālam*.
bridle-path, *kudiräi-p-pādäi*.
bright, *piragāçamāṉa*.
bring, *konḍu vā*.
bring forth, *peṟu, īṉu*.
brink, *viḷimbu; ōram*.
broad, *agalamāṉa*.
brook, *çiṯṯāṟu*.
brother, *çagōdaraṉ*.
bud, n., *tuḷir, pū-moṭṭu*.
build, v., *kaṭṭu*.
bund (of a tank), *karäi*.
bundle, *poṭṭaṇam; kaṭṭu*.
bungalow, *baṅgaḷā*.
burn, v. intr., *vē, aṟalu; tr., çuḍu*.
burst, *uḍäi, veḍi*.

bury, *pudäi; adakkam pannu.*
bush, *çedi; pudar.*
bushel, *buçal, pushal.*
business, *vēläi, aluval.*
but, *ānālum*; (except) *tavira.*
butt, v., *muttu, tākku.*
butter-dish, *venney pāttiram.*
buy, *viläikku vāngu.*
by, *-āl, kondu.*

Cage, *kūdu.*
calamity, *ābattu.*
calculate, *ennu, kanakk' idu.*
call, v., *kūppidu; arüi.*
camphor, *karppūram.*
can, v., *kūdum.*
cane, n., *pirambu.*
cannot, *kūdādu; ēlādu.*
capital (money), *kaimudal.*
captive, *çiräi, adimäi.*
car, *iratam, tēr.*
card, *çīttu.*
care, n., *vaçam, pattiram, kavanam, kariçanäi.*
carry away, *çumandu pō; kondu pō.*
cart-road, *karattäi rōttu* or *vīdi.*
cartridge, *tōttā.*
case (box), *petti;* (cover) *uräi.*
— (in law), *varakku.*
cash, *kāçu; çalli.*
cash-box, *kāçup-petti.*
cask, *pīppā.*
cast forth, *eri, vīçu.*
caste, *çādi (jāti), kulam.*
catch, v., *pidi, pattu.*
cattle, *ādumādu.*
cattle-keeper, *māttukkāran.*
cattle-shed (or fold), *māttu-p-patti.*
cause, n., *kāranam.*

cave, *kebi; kugäi.*
cease, *aru; ōy; ori; ninru pō.*
centre, *nadu; matti.*
cereals, *tāniya vagäi.*
ceremony, *çadangu.*
certain, *niccayamāna.*
certainty, *niccayam, niçam.*
chaff, *padar, çāvi.*
chain, *çangili; todarcci.*
chalk, *çīmäic-cunnāmbu.*
change, n., *vērupādu, mārudal;* v.intr., *māru, tiri;* v.tr., *māttu.*
chapter, *adigāram.*
charge, n. & v. (accuse), *kuttañ çāttu.*
charge (care), n., *vaçam, poruppu.*
charge (a price), v., *viläi çol.*
cheap, a., *malivāna, nayamāna.*
cheat, v., *mōçam pannu.*
check, v., *tadu.*
cheerful, *çandōshamāna.*
chess, *çaturangam, çokkattān.*
chew, v., *mellu.*
chief, a., *piradāna;* n., *mudalāli, piradāni.*
chief justice, *nītiyadipati.*
chili pepper, *koccik-kāy, paccäi-mila-kāy.*
chill, n., *kulir.*
chip, n., *çimbu, çirāy.*
chisel, n., *uli.*
cholera, *visha pēdi.*
choose, *terind' edu.*
chop, v., *vettu; tari.*
cigar, *çuruttu.*
cinder, *taral.*
cinnamon, *karuvā-p-pattai.*
circle, *vattam; viruttam.*
cistern, *totti.*
city, *nagaram.*

civil case, *çivil-vaṛakku*.
civility, *mariyādäi*.
claim, n., *urimai*.
class, n., *vagäi, vaguppu*.
clay, *kaḷi-maṇ*.
clean, *çuttamāṉa*.
clear, a., *teḷivāṉa*.
clearly, *teḷivāy*.
cleave, v., *piḷa*.
cleft, n., *piḷappu*.
clever, *keṭṭiyāṉa*.
climb, v., *ēṟu*.
cling, v., *oṭṭik-koḷ, paṯṯippiḍi*.
clip, v., *kattari*.
close, adv. (densely), *aḍartti-yāy*.
close, v., *mūḍu; aḍäi*.
close (near), a., *kiṭṭa, aḍutta*.
closet, *uḷḷaṟäi; ciṯṯaṟäi*.
clothe, v., *uḍu; uḍuttu*.
club (wooden), *taḍi, daṇḍu*.
coarse, *parumpaḍiyāṉa, muradāṉa, iṟivāṉa*.
coffee bush, *kōppi-ç-çeḍi*.
coffee estate, *kōppi-t-tōṭṭam*.
coffin, *çavappeṭṭi*.
coin, n., *nāṇayam, paṇam*; v. (coin money), *kāç'aḍi*.
cold, a., *kuḷircciyāṉa*.
collect, v.intr., *kūḍu, tiraḷu*; v.tr., *kūṭṭu, çēr*.
college, *kalvi-ç-çālāi*.
colt, *kuṭṭi*.
come, *vā*.
comfortable, *vaçadiyāṉa*.
command, n., *kaṭṭaḷäi, ēval, uttaravu*; v., *kaṭṭaḷäi-y-iḍu*.
commencement, *toḍakkam, ārambam*.
commerce, n., *viyāpāram, varttagam*.
common, *poduvāṉa*.

commotion, *kalakkam*.
compact, adj., *aḍakkamāṉa*.
companion, *kūṭṭāḷi*.
compare, *ottu-p-pār*.
compartment, *aṟäi*.
complain, *muṟäiyiḍu*.
complainant, *vādi*.
complete, v., *muḍi, tīr, niṟai*.
completely, *muṯṯilum, muṟu-vadum*.
completeness, *pūraṇam*.
completion, *niṟäivu, tīrppu*.
condition, *taṉmäi, niläimäi*.
conduct, n., *naḍakkäi*.
conduct, v., *naḍattu*, (escort) *tuṇäi pō*.
confidence, *nambikkäi*.
confusion, *kalakkam, kuṛap-pam*.
congregation, *çabäi*.
connection, *çambandam*.
conscience, *maṉaç-çātci*.
consent, n., *içäivu, anumadi*; v., *içäi*.
consider, *niṉäi*.
consign, *oppuk-koḍu*.
consult, *uçāvu*.
consultation, *ālōçaṉäi*. [yam.
contentment, *maṉa-rammi-*
contents, *aḍakkam, poṛippu*.
continually, *aḍikkaḍi, nitti-yamum*.
contract, n., *uḍaṉpaḍikkäi, poruttam*; v. (shrink), *kuṟäi, çuruṅgu*.
contractor, *poruttakkāraṉ*.
contradict, *maṟu, edirttu-p-pēçu*
cook, n., *kuçiṉikkāraṉ, kōkki*.
cook, v., *çamäi, pāgam paṇṇu*,
coolie, *kūlikkāraṉ; kūliyāḷ*.
cork, *kuccu*.
correct, v., *tiruttu*.
correct, a., *tiṭṭamāṉa, çariyāṉa*.

cost, *kirayam; viläi; çelavu.*
cottage, *kudiçäi.*
cough, v., *irumu*; n., *irumal.*
count, v., *ennu.*
country, *nādu, dēçam.*
court, *kōrttu, nītistalam.*
cover, v., *mūdu;* n., *mūdi, urāi.*
criminal, *kuttavāli.*
cripple, *çappāni, nondi.*
crooked, *kōnalāna.*
cross, a. (athwart) & n., *kurukku.*
crowbar, *kadappārāi alavāngu.*
crowd, *çanakkūttam.*
cruelty, *kodumäi, kurūram.*
cry, v., *çattam-pōdu; aru.*
cultivate, *payir-idu.*
culvert, *madagu, vārāvadi.*
cunning, n., *agadavigadam.*
cunning, a., *tandiramāna.*
cure, v., *çugappaduttu.*
current, a., *çellum.*
current (month), *nāladu.*
current (stream), *ōttam.*
curry, *kari.*
curse, v., *çabi;* n., *çābam.*
custom, *varakkam.*
cut, v., *ari; vettu.*
cut (reap), *aru.*
cut down, *tari.*
cutting, n., *arivu, vettu.*

Daily, *nāl tōrum (nādorum).*
damage, n., *çēdam.*
damp, *īram.*
dance, v., *ādu.*
dancing girl, *nadanamādu, tēvadiyāl.*
dangerous, *mōçamāna.*
dark, to become, *iruttu.*
darkness, *irul.*
date, *tēdi.*

dawn, v., *vidi;* n., *vidiyat kālam.*
day and night, *allum pagalum.*
deafness, *çevidu.*
dear (costly), *viläiyulla, arumäiyāna.*
dear, *piriyamulla.*
death, *maranam, irappu.*
debt, *kadan.*
decay, v., *arugip-pō.*
deceit, *vañjanäi.*
decide, *tīr; tīrmāni.*
decrease, v., *kuräi, kuräindup-pō.*
deduct, *kari.*
deep, a., *āramāna.*
defendant, *piradivādi; edirāli.*
defraud, *vañji, abagari.*
delay, n., *tāmadam.*
delight, n., *inbam.*
deliver, *tappuvi; iratci.*
dense, *çerivulla, ganatta, adarttiyāna.*
deny, *maru.*
depart, *purappadu, pōy vidu.*
depth, *āram, pallam.*
descend, *irangu.*
desert (wilderness), *vanāntaram, pārnilam.*
desire, *āçäi.*
desire, v., *āçäi-p-padu, virumbu.*
destitute person, *agadi.*
destroy, *kedu, ari.*
destruction, *arivu, kēdu.*
detain, *mari, tadu.*
devour, *patci; virungu.*
die, *çā; çettu-p-pō; ira.*
difference, *bēdam, vittiyāçam.*
dig, *tōndu.*
digest, v., *çami.*
diligently, *çuruçuruppāy.*
diminish, *kuräi.*
dip, v., *tōy.*
direct, v. (order), *kattalāiyidu;* (guide) *vari kāttu.*

dirt (filth), *arukku.*
disappear, *marai.*
disgrace, n., *avamānam.*
disgust, n., *veruppu*; v., *veru.*
dishonesty, *kapadam, tirut-tuttanam.*
dismiss, *talli-vidu.*
disobedience, *kīrppadiyāmäi.*
dispute, n., *varakku, vādam*; v., *tarkki.*
dissolve, *urugu, karäi.*
distance, *tūram, toläi.*
distinctly, *telivāy.*
distress, *varuttam*; *tunbam.*
distribute, *pangidu.*
distrust, n., *çamuçayam, ava-nambikkäi.*
ditch, *pallam, agar.*
dive, v., *mukkuli, mūrgu.*
diver, *kulikāran.*
divide, *pang'idu*; *piri.*
division, *pirivu, pangu, pagu-* [*di*
do, *çey, pannu.*
doubt, n., *çandēgam.*
down, adv., *kīrē*; *paniya.*
drain, *kālvāy*; *tūmbu.*
drain, v., *vadi.*
drama, *nādagam, vilāçam.*
draw, v., *iru.*
dream, n., *çoppanam, kanavu.*
drink, v., *kudi.*
drive, v,, *ōttu.*
driver, *pāgan, ōttugiravan.*
drizzle, *tūttal.*
drop, n. & v., *tuli.*
drop, v., *kīrē vidu.* [*varatçi*
drought, *marai illāmäi,*
drum (tom-tom), *tamukku, pa-*
drunk, *veritta, veriyāna.* [*räi.*
drunkard, *veriyan, kudiyan.*
dry, *kāynda.*
dry (to become), *kāy, ularu.*
due, *kadanāna, uriya, tagunda.*
dull, *mandam-ulla, marunga-*
dumb, a., *ūmäiyāna.* [*lāna.*
durable, *urudiyāna.*
during, *varäiyil, porudu.*
dust, *tūl, tūçi.*
duty, *kadamäi.*
dwell, *kudiyiru.* [*çāyan-tōy.*
dye, n., *çāyam, niram*; v.,

Each, *ovvoru.*
early, *kālamē.*
earn, *çambādi.*
earthquake, *pūmi-y-adircci.*
easy, *ilēçāna.*
eat, *çāppidu, tin, un.*
edge, *ōram*; *kūr.*
educate, *padippi*; *katpi.*
effort, *muyatci, utçāgam.*
either...or, *āvadu.*
elder (man), *mūttavan.*
— (woman), *mūttaval.*
elevate, *uyarttu, ēttu.*
elsewhere, *vērengē-yāvadu.*
embark, *kappal ēru.*
embezzle, *kavar, kalavu çey.*
embrace, *taruvu, anäi.*
empire, *irājjiyam.*
employ, v., *ētpaduttu, vēläi kol.*
employment, *vēläi*; *aluval.*
empty, *verumäiyāna.* [*ullidu.*
enclose, *adakkan çey*; *adäi*;
enclosure wall, *çuttu-ç-çuvar.*
end, v., *mudi.* [*arudi.*
end, n., *mudivu*; *kadäiçi*;
endeavour, v., *pirayattanam pannu.*
enemy, *virōdi, çatturu.*
engage (for service), *vēläikku*
enough, *pōdum.* [*amarttu.*

enquire, *viçāri.*
enter, *piravēçi; pugu.*
entirely, *muṟudum, muḻḻilum.*
envy, n., *poṟāmäi.*
equal, a., *çamāṉamāṉa, çama.*
erect, v., *nimirttu.*
err, *tavaṟu.*
error, *piṛäi.*
escape, v., *tappi-k-koḷ, vilagi-p-pō.*
establish, *stābi.*
estate (riches), *āsti.*
estate (land), *nilam, tōṭṭam.*
et cætera, *ādi, mudaliya.*
event, *çaṅgadi, naḍanda kāriyam.*
every, *ovvoru.*
evidence, *vākkumūlam, çāṭci.*
evident, *pirattiyaṭcamāṉa, teḷivāṉa.*
evil, n., *tīmäi, dōsham;* a., *tīya, keṭṭa.*
exact, a., *tiṭṭamāṉa.*
exaggerate, *pārāṭṭu.*
examine, *çōdi, parīṭci.*
example, *mādiri, udāraṇam.*
excavate, *kuḍäi.*
except, prep., *tavira.*
exclude, *vilakku, nīkki viḍu.*
excuse, n., *pōkku, çākku;* v., *maṉṉi, piṛäi poṟu.*
exercise, n., *appiyāçam, paṟakkam.*
expect, *edirpār, nambu.*
expense, *çelavu.*
expert, a., *paṛagiṉa, cāmarttiyamuḷḷa.*
explain, *vistari, viḷakku.*
extend, *nīṭṭu.*
extent, *aḷavu, viçālam.*

Fable, *kadäi, kaṭṭukkadäi.*
fact, *mey, uṇmäi.*
fade, *vāḍi-p-pō.*
fail, *piçagu.*
faint, *çōrndu-p-pō.*
faith, *viçuvāçam, batti.*
fall, v., *viṛu;* n., *vīṛvu.*
fall off (as leaves), *udiru.*
false, *poyyāṉa.*
falsehood, *poy.*
famine, *pañjam, karuppu.*
fan, n., *viçiṟi;* v., *viçiṟu.*
fast, a. (swift), *viräivāṉa;* (firm) *tiḍamāṉā.*
fasten, *pūṭṭu.*
fat, a., *pushṭiyuḷḷa, koṛutta.*
fatigue, n., *iḷäippu;* v., *iḷäi.*
fault, *tappu, kuṯṯam.*
favour, n., *dayavu.*
fear, n., *payam;* v., *payappaḍu, añju.*
feast, n., *virundu, paṇḍigäi.*
feather, *iṟagu.*
fee, *kūli, çambaḷam.*
feeble, *noyya, balavīṉamāṉa.*
feed, v., *tiṉ; mēy, bōjaṉaṅ koḍu.*
feel, *uṇar.*
feeling, *uṇarvu, ūṟu.*
fertile, *çeṛippuḷḷa.*
fetch, *pōyi-k-koṇḍu vā.*
few, *çila, koñja.*
fiddle, *kiṉṉaram, vīṇäi.*
fight, v., *çaṇḍäi çey, pōr-āḍu;* n., *çaṇḍäi.*
file, n., *aram.*
fill, v.tr., *nirappu;* v.intr., *nirambu.*
find, *kaṇḍu piḍi.*
fine, a., *melliya, nērttiyāṉa.*
fine, n. (penalty), *taṇḍam.*
finish, v.tr., *muḍi, tīr;* n., *muḍivu, muṭṭu.*
fire (a gun), v., *veḍi çuḍu.*
firm, *niläiyāṉa, stiramāṉa.*

fit, a., *takka, ēṯṯa.*
fit, v.intr., *porundu;* v.tr., *içäi, poruttu.*
fitness, *tagudi.*
fix, *nāṭṭu, niṟuttu.*
flag (banner), *koḍi.*
flat, *taṭṭäiyāṉa.*
flea, *teḷḷu.*
flesh, *taçäi; māmiçam.*
float, v., *mida, nīndu.*
flood, *veḷḷam.*
flow, v., *ōḍu, ūṟu.*
flow (of the tide), *ēṯṯam.*
fly, v., *paṟa;* n., *ī.*
fold (cattle), *āttukkiḍäi.*
fold, v., *maḍi.*
follow, *piṉ çel* or *toḍar.*
fool, *mūḍaṉ, maḍäiyaṉ.*
forbid, *vilakku, taḍu.*
force, n., *palam.* [*tāṇḍu.*
ford, n., *kaḍakkiṟa tuṟäi;* v.,
foreign, *aṉṉiya, puṟambāṉa.*
forget, *maṟa.*
forgive, *maṉṉi.*
forgiveness, *maṉṉippu.*
form, n., *uruvam;* v., *paḍäi, uruvākku.*
former, *mundiṉa, pūrva.*
forth, adv., *veḷiyē.*
fortress, *kōṭṭäi.*
forward, adv., *muṉṉē.*
foundation, *astivāram.*
fountain, *ūṯṯu.*
fresh, a., *pudiya; paccäi.*
friend, *çinēgidaṉ.*
front, *muṉ.*
fry, *pori.*
fuel, *viṟagu.*
full, *niṟäivāṉa.*
funeral, *iḻavu, aḍakkam.*
furnace, *çūḷäi; kugäi.*

further, adv., *mēlum, iṉṉam.*
future, *iṉimēl, varuṅkālam.*

Gain, *ādāyam.*
gain, v., *çambādi, ādāyam*
gamble, *çūd'āḍu.* [*paṇṇu.*
gambling, *çūdu.*
gang, *kūṭṭam, çaṅgam.*
gardener, *tōṭṭakkāraṉ.*
gather, *kūṭṭu; çēr.*
gem, *maṇi.*
general, a., *poduvāṉa.*
gentle, *çāduvāṉa.*
gentleman, *turäi.*
get, *çambādi, peṟu, vāṅgu.*
gift, *iṉām, īgäi.*
gimlet, *tuṟappaṇam.*
give, *ī, iḍu, koḍu.*
glad, *çandoshamāṉa.*
glass (substance), *paḷiṅgu,*
gnaw, *kaḍi; ari.* [*kaṇṇāḍi.*
go, *pō.*
good, *nalla.*
goods, *cāmāṉ, çarakku.*
government, *çarkkār.*
gradually, *paḍippaḍiyāy.*
grain, *dāṉiyam.*
grand, *perumäiyāṉa.*
grant, v., *aruḷu, koḍu;* n., *īgäi.*
grasp, n. & v., *paṯṟu, piḍi.*
gratis, *ilavaçamāy.*
grave, n., *pirēdak-kuḻi.*
graze, *mēy.*
grease, n., *koḻuppu.*
great, *periya.*
grief, *dukkam, kavaläi.*
grey, *naräitta.*
grind, v., *aräi.*
grindstone, *ammi, çāṇäi.*
ground, *nilam; taräi.*
grove, *çōläi; tōppu*

grow, *vaḷar.*
growl, v., *uṟumu.*
grumble, *muṟumuṟu.*
guard, v., *kā;* n., *kāval.*
guardian, *kāvalaṉ.*
guest, *viruntaṉ.*
guide, v., *vaḻi kāṭṭu;* n., *vaḻi-*
guilt, *kuṭṭam.* [*kāṭṭi.*
gum, *īṟu, piçiṉ.*
gun, *tubākki, veḍitōkku.*
gunpowder, *veḍi-marundu.*

Habit, *vaḻakkam.*
half, *arāi.*
hall, n., *çālāi.*
hamlet, *çiṭṭūr, kuppam.*
hammer, *çuttiyal.* [*tūkku.*
hang, v.intr., *toṅgu;* v.tr.,
happen, *nēriḍu; naḍa.*
happily, *adiṭṭamāy, anukūla-*
happiness, *pākkiyam.* [*māy.*
happy, *pākkiyamāṉa.*
hard, *kaḍiṉamāṉa.*
harm, n., *tīṅgu; keḍudi.*
harvest, *aṟuppu.*
haste, *çuṟukku, turidam.*
hatchet, *kai-k-kōḍāli.*
have, *vaitt' iru; aḍaind' iru.*
hawker, *poṭṭanikkāraṉ.*
he, *avaṉ.*
heal, *çugap-paḍuttu.*
heap, v., *aḍukku;* n., *kuviyal.*
hear, *kēḷ.*
hearing, *kēḷvi.*
heavy, *pāramāṉa.*
hedge, *vēli.*
heifer, *kiḍāri.*
height, *uyaram.*
heir, *urimāikkāraṉ.* [*udavu.*
help, n., *ottāçāi, udavi;* v.,
hemp, *çaṇal; çaṇappu.*

hence, *iṅgē yirundu.*
henceforth, *idumudal, iṉimēl.*
herd, *mandāi.*
here, *iṅgē.*
hereafter, *iṉimēl.*
hereabout, *indappakkattilē,*
  iṅṅaṉam, kiṭṭa.
herb, *pūṇḍu, kīrāi.*
hereby, *idiṉāl.*
herewith, *ittuḍaṉ, idōḍu.*
hesitate, *aiyappaḍu.*
hew, *veṭṭu; taṟi.*
hide, v., *maṟāi;* n., *tōl.*
high, *uyaramāṉa, mēlāṉa.*
hinge, *kīl.* [*vāṅgu.*
hire, n., *kūli:* v., *kūlikku*
hitherto, *iduvarāikkum, im-*
  maṭṭum.
hive (bee-), *tēṉkūḍu.*
hold, v., *piḍi; kol.* [*māṉa.*
hollow, a., *kuṟalāṉa; paḷḷa-*
hollow, n., *kuṟal, paḷḷam.*
holy, *tiru, pariçudda.*
home, *vīḍu.* [*yāṉa.*
honest, *nērmāiyuḷḷa, unmāi-*
honesty, *unmāi; nērmāi.*
honey, *tēṉ.*
honour, *māṉam, pūjāi.*
honourable (in addressing),
  irāyastiri; kaṉam-uḷḷa.
hook, n., *tūṇḍil, koḷuvi;* v.,
  māṭṭu, koḷuvu.
hope, n., *nambikkāi;* v., *nambu.*
horn, *kombu.*
horsekeeper, *kudirāi-k-kāraṉ.*
horse-shoe, *lāḍam.*
hospital, *āspattiri.*
hot, *çūḍāṉa; kāramāṉa.*
hot season, *kōḍāi-k-kālam.*
how, *eppaḍi.*
how many, *ettaṉāi.*

how much, *evvalavu.*
hunger, *paçi.*
hungry, *paçiyuḷḷa.*
hunt, n., *vēṭṭäi*; v., *vēṭṭäiyāḍu.*
hurt, *nōgappaṇṇu.*
husk, *umi*; *ōḍu.*
hut, *kuḍiçäi.*

I, *nāṉ.*
idea, *abippirāyam.*
idiot, *payittiyakkāraṉ.*
idle, *çōmbāṉa.*
idleness, *çōmbal*; *ālaçiyam.*
if, *āṉāl.*
ignorance, *aññāṉam.*
image, *çāyal*, *çurūpam.*
imitate, *pōla-ç-çey.*
immediately, *uḍaṉē.*
immovable, *açäivaṯṯa.*
impatience, *poṟāmäi.*
imperfect, *kuṟäivāṉa.*
important, *piradāṉa.*
improper, *tagāda.*
improve, v.intr., *tirundu*; v.tr., *tiruttu.*
impudent, *tuḍukkāṉa.*
impurity, *açuddam.*
incessant, *ōyāda.*
inch, *aṅgulam.*
income, *varavu*, *ādāyam.*
increase, v., *adigari*; *perugu.*
incurable, *açāttiya.*
indebted, *kaḍaṉ paṭṭa.*
india-rubber, *rappar.*
indigo, *avuri.*
industry, *muyaṯçi*, *ūkkam.*
infant, *kuḻandäi.*
inform, *teriyappaḍuttu.*
inhabit, *kuḍiyiru.*
inhabitant, *kuḍiyāṉavaṉ.*
injustice, *aniyāyam.*
inquire, *viçāri*; *kēḷ.*
insensible, *uṇarcciyillāda.*
insert, *iḍäiyilē çēr.*
inside, *uṭpuṟam.*
inspect, *çōdi.*
inspection, *pariçōdaṉäi.*
instead, *padilāga.*
instruct, *pōdi*; *paḍippi.*
instrument, *āyudam*; *karuvi.*
insubordinate, *kīḻppaḍiyāda.*
insufficient, *pōdāda.*
insult, n., *avamāṉam*, *nindäi.*
intention, *çindäi*, *nōkkam.*
interpreter, *tuppāçi.*
invite, *aḻäi.*
inward, *uḷḷāṉa.*
iron, a., *iruppu*; n., *irumbu.*
irrigate, *nīr pāyccu.*
is, *uṇḍu.*
it, *adu.*

Jackal, *nari.*
jail, *maṟiyal-vīḍu*; *çiṟäi-ç-çālāi.*
jar, *jāḍi.*
jealousy, *ericcal*, *erivu.*
jest, *parigāçam*, *kēli.*
jewel, *nagäi*; *ābaraṇam.*
join, v.tr., *çēr*, *iṇäi*; v.intr., *çēr*, *kūḍu*, *porundu.*
joint, n., *poruttu*; *kaṇu*; *kulāiccu.*
joy, *kaḷippu.*
judge, n., *nītipati*; *nītivāṉ.*
judgment (decision), *tīrppu.*
juice, *çāram.*
jump, *kudi.*
junction, *çandi.*
jungle, *kāḍu.*
jury, *yūrimār*; *pañçāyattār naḍuttīrväi.*
justice, *niyāyam.*

Keep, *vai*; *kā.*
kick, v. & n., *udäi.*

kill, *kolāi çey; kol.*
kiln, *cūḷāi.*
kind, n. (sort), *iṉam, vagāi.*
kind, a., *dayāiyuḷḷa.*
kindle, v., *mūḷu, tīppaṯṯu.*
kindness, *dayavu; paṭcam.*
king, *irājā, araçaṉ.*
kingdom, *irājjiyam; araçu.*
kite (hawk), *parundu*; (toy) *paṭṭam.*
kitten, *pūṉāik-kuṭṭi.*
knock, v., *aḍi; taṭṭu.*
knot, *muḍiççu.*
know, v., *aṟi.*
knowledge, *aṟivu.*

Labour, *vēlāi; pirayāçam.*
labourer, *kūliyāḷ.*
lad, *poḍiyaṉ.*
ladder, *ēṇi.*
ladle, *agappāi.*
lady, *turāi-çāṉi.*
lameness, *muḍam.*
language, *bāshāi.*
lantern, *lantar; dīpakkūḍu.*
lap, *maḍi.*
lap, v., *nakku.*
large, *periya; parutta.*
last, a., *kaḍāiçiyāṉa.*
last, v., *tangu, nāṭpaḍu.*
latch, *kadavu māṭṭi.*
late, adv., *pindi.*
late, *pindiṉa*; (deceased) *māji, iṟandū pōṉa.*
lath, *variccu.* [*rippu.*
laugh, v., *çiri; nagāi*; n., *çi-*
law, *kaṭṭaḷāi, vidi, nīti; çaṭ-*
lay, v., *vai.* [*ṭam.*
lead (metal), n., *īyam.*
lead, v., *mundi-p-pō; naḍattu.*
leaf, *ilāi.*

leak, n., *oḻukku.*
lean, a., *melinda.*
lean, v., *çāy, çār.*
leanness, *melivu.*
leap, v., *pāy: kudi.*
learn, *paḍi, kal.*
leave, v., *viṭṭuppō*; n., *viḍāi,*
leech, *aṭṭāi.* [*uttaravu.*
left (side), *iḍadu.*
leisure, *çāvagāçam.*
lend, *iraval koḍu.*
length, *nīḷam.*
lessen, *kuṟāi.*
lesson, *pāḍam.*
let, v., *viḍu.* [n., *maṭṭam.*
level, v., *niravu, çamam-ākku;*
liberty, *viḍudalāi.*
lick, v., *nakku.*
lie down, v., *paḍu.*
lie (to speak falsehood), *poy-*
life, *uyir, jīvaṉ.* [*çol.*
lift, v., *tūkku; eḍu.*
light, a., *ilēçāṉa.*
like, a., *pōl; otta.*
lime (slaked), *çuṇṇāmbu.*
lime (fruit), *tēçik-kāy: elumic-cam-paḻam.*
lime-squeezer, *tēçikkāy iḍukki.*
limestone, *çukkāṉ kal.*
limit, n., *maṭṭu, ellāi.*
line (row), *nirāi*; (stroke) *irēkāi, kīṟu, vari*: (cord) *kayiṟu*; (thread) *nūl.*
linger, *tāmadappaḍu.*
link (of a chain), *çangili-valāiyam*; v., *piṇāi.*
lintel, *mēl nilāi.*
list (schedule), n., *çābidā, aṭṭavaṇāi.*
listen, *uṯṯu-k-kēḷ.*
little, *çiṉṉa çiṟu.*

live, a., *uyirulla.*
live, v., *çīvi; pirāi; vaçi.*
load, n., *pāram, çumäi;* v., *pāramēttu, çumattu.*
loam, *paçalāi-man.*
locust, *vettukkili.*
long, a., *nīlamāna, nīnda, nedu;* v., *āçi, icci.*
longing, *āçäi.*
look, v., *nōkku, pār.*
loop, *kuräiccu.*
loose, *avirnda; talarttiyāna.*
loose (untie), v., *avir.*
lop, v., *tari, vettu.*
lord (master), *āndavar.*
lose, *ira; irandu pō.*
loss, *iravu, pādu.*
lot (share), *paṅgu, vīdam.*
lotus, *tāmaräi.*
loudly, *urattu, urakka.*
love, n., *anbu, nēçam;* v., *anbu vai, nēçi, virumbu.*
low, *kīrāna, tārnda.*
lower, v.tr., *irakku;* intr., *tār.*
lump, n., *katti.*

Mace (spice), *çādippattiri.*
machine, *çūttiram.*
mad, *payittiya; unmatta.*
madam, *ammäi, eçamāni.*
magistrate, *niyāyādipati.*
maim, v., *ūnappaduttu.*
make, v., *pannu.*
— (cause to become), *ākku.*
Maldive fish, *māçi.*
male, n. & a., *ān.*
mallet, *kottān.*
manage, *kaiyālu, nadappi.*
mango tree, *māmaram.*
mango fruit, *mām param.*
manliness, *ānmäi.*
manner, *mādiri, vidam; vagäi.*
manners, good, *nallorukkam.*
mansion, *māligäi.*
manufacture, *kaittoril.*
manure, n., *eru, uram.*
many, *anēga, pala, vegu.*
map, *dēça-p-padam.*
mare, *pettäi-k-kudiräi.*
margosa, *vēmbu.*
margosa leaves, *vēpp'ilāi.*
mark, *kuri; adäiyālam.*
mark, v., *adäiyālam pōdu.*
marriage, *kaliyānam.*
master, *eçamān, vātti.*
matter, n., *porul; çaṅgadi.*
mattock (mamatty), *manvetti.*
mature, v., *paru.*
maturity, *pakkuvam.*
meal (flour), *mā.*
mean (low), *nīça, atpamānā.*
mean, v., *karudu.*
meaning, *karuttu; aruttam.*
meanness, *nīçam, piçunam.*
measure, n., *alavu.*
measure, v., *ala.*
meet, v., *çandi, edirppadu.*
meeting, *kūttam; çaṅgam.*
melt, *karäi; urugu.*
member (of the body, etc.), *avayavam.*
memorandum, *iyādāstu.*
memory, *ñābagam; yādi.*
mend, *parudu pār.*
mention, *çol, arivi.*
merchandise, *viyābāram; çarakku.*
merchant, *varttagan; viyābāri.*
mercy, *irakkam.*
method, *oruṅgu; vidam.*
middle, *nadu.*
midst, n., *nadu; maiyam.*

midway, adv., *iḍäirariyil.*
mildness, *çāndam.*
mind, n., *maṉam.*
mine, n., *çuraṅgam, kaṉi.*
mineral, *niraça vastu.*
mingle, *kala, tōy.*
minute (tiny), *nuṭpamāṉa.*
mischief, *kuṟumbu; tīṅgu.*
misery, *nirppandam.*
misfortune, *iḍäiyūṟu, ābattu.*
miss, v., *piçagu.*
mistake, n., *piḻäi, tappidam.*
mistress, *eçamāṭṭi.*
mix, v., *kala.*
mixture, *kalappu.*
model, n., *mādiri.*
moisture, *paçäi, īram.*
more, *adiga; iṉṉam.*
mortar, *ural*; (cement) *çāṇḍu.*
mosque, *paḷḷivāçal.*
moss, *pāçi.*
moth, *pūcci, puṟu.*
motive, *kāraṇam, nōkkam*
mould, n., *accu, karu.*
mound, *mēḍu, tiḍal.*
mount, v., *ēṟu.*
mourn, v., *tukkaṅ koṇḍāḍu.*
move, v., *açäi; āḍu.*
mow (cut), *aṟu*; *veṭṭu.* [*ba.*
much, *adigam; migudi*; *rem-*
mud, *çēṟu; çagadi.* [*agaṉ.*
Mohammedan, *tulukkaṉ, çōṉ-*
multiply, v.tr., *perukku, adi-*
gari; intr., *perugu.*
murder, *koläi.*
music, *çaṅgīdam.*
must, *vēṇḍum.*
myself, *nāṉē.*

Nail, *āṇi;* (finger-) *nagam.*
name, n., *pēr;* v., *peyar-iḍu.*

narrowness, *iḍukkam.*
native, n., *çudēçi.*
nature, *iyalbu.*
near, *kiṭṭa.*
near at hand, *aṇḍäiyil.*
nearly, *koñjaṅ kuṟäiya.*
nearness, *çamībam.*
necessity, *avaçiyam, tēväi.*
needle, *ūçi.*
neglect, n., *açaṭṭäi; kavaläi-*
neighbour, *ayalāṉ.* [*yīṉam.*
neighbourhood, *ayal.*
nest, *kūḍu.*
net, *valäi.*
never, *orukkālum illäi.*
new, *pudu.*
news, *çeydi.*
next, a., *aḍutta*; adv., *aḍukka.*
nibble, n., *ari.*
nip, v., *kiḷḷu.*
no, *illäi.*
noise, *çattam; iräiccal.*
nonsense, *puttiyīṉam.*
noose, *çurukku, pāçam.*
nor, *āvadu.*
north, n., *vaḍakku.*
north wind, *vāḍäi.*
north-east monsoon, *piṉ-māri-*
kālam; piçāṉa kālam.
nostril, *mūkku-t-tuvāram.*
not, *illäi; alla.*
note (memo), *kuṟippu;* (letter)
note, v., *kuṟittu vai.* [*çīṭṭu.*
nothing, *oṉṟum illäi.*
notice, *arivittal; arikkäi.*
notice, v., *kavaṉi; pār.*
notion, *eṇṇam.*
now, *ippoḻudu; ippō.*
nowadays, *innāṭkaḷil.*
nowhere, *ōriḍattilum illäi.*
number, *ilakkam.*

number, v., *eṇṇu.*
nut, *koṭṭäi.*

Oar, *taṇḍu, tuḍuppu.*
oath, *āṇäi.*
obedience, *kīrppaḍidal.*
object, *viçayam, nōkkam.*
object, v., *taḍu; āṭcēbi.*
objection, *āṭcēbam; taḍäi.*
observance, *āçāram.*
obstruct, *vari-y-aḍäi, mari.*
obstruction, *aḍaippu.*
obtain, *aḍäi, peṟu, kiḍäi.*
occasion, *vēḷäi; tarunam.*
occasionally, *iḍäikkiḍäiyē.*
occupation, *vēläi, toril.*
occupy, *kuḍiyiru, vāçam paṇṇu*
odour, *vāçanäi; maṇam.*
off, *tūra; vilaga.*
offence, *kuṭṭam, kuṟäi.*
offend, *anāçāram paṇṇu.*
office (room), *āpiçu; uttiyōga çāläi.*
office (berth), *uttiyōgam.*
often, *aḍikkaḍi.*
oil, *eṇṇäi.*
old, *paṛäiya.*
old man, *kiṛavan.*
old woman, *kiṛavi.*
omit, *viṭṭu viḍu.*
on, *mēlē.*
once, *orutaram; oruviçäi.*
only, *māttiram.*
open, v., *tiṟa.*
order (command), *kaṭṭaläi; (regularity) variçäi; oruṅgu.*
order, v., *ākkiyābi.*
origin, *mūlam.*
ornament, *aṇi; alaṅgāram.*
orphan, *peṯṟār illāda piḷḷäi.*
other, *maṟu, maṯṟa.*

ought, *vēṇḍum.*
out, *puṟambē.*
outward, *puṟambāna.*
oval, a., *muṭṭäi vaḍivāna.*
over, *mēl.*
overcharge, v., *adiga-viläi-pōḍu.*
overflow, *tadumbu; karäipu-raṇḍ'ōḍu.*
overlook (neglect), *pārāmal viḍu;* (look over) *mēlviçāri.*
overseer, *kaṅgāṇi.*
overtake, *toḍarndu piḍi.*
owe, *kaḍan paṭṭ'iru.*
own, a., *tan, çonda.*
own, v., *urimäi-y-ākku.*
owner, *condakkāran, uḍäiyavan.*

Pace (step), *naḍäi.*
pack (sack), *podi.*
pack, v., *aḍukku.*
pack-bullock, *podi-māḍu.*
package, *kaṭṭu.*
page (of a book), *pakkam.*
paint, n., *varṇam.*
paint, v., *varṇi; varṇam pūçu.*
pane of glass, *kaṇṇāḍit taṭṭu.*
panel, *aḍäippalagäi.*
pardon, n., *mannippu.*
parents, *peṯṟōr.*
part, n., *paṅgu.*
part, v., *paṅg'iḍu; pirindu pō.*
partiality, *paṭcapādam.*
party, n., *kūṭṭam; paṭçattār.*
pass (away), *kari, nīṅgu.*
pass (current), v., *çel.*
pass over, v., *kaḍandu pō.*
passenger, *varippōkkan.*
pasture, *mēyccal.*
pat, v., *taṭṭu.*
patience, *poṟumäi.*
pave, *kaṭpāvu.*

paw, *kāl kai.*
pawn (pledge), n., *aḍagu ; v., aḍagu vai.*
pay, v., *çēluttu, çambaḷam koḍu;* n., *çambalam.*
peace, *camādāṉam.*
pea-fowl, *mayil.*
peculiar, *viçēçamāṉa.*
peel, peel off, v., *uri.*
peep, v., *eṭṭi-p-pār; oṭṭi-p-pār.*
peg, n., *muḷai, āppu.*
penalty, *daṇḍam.*
people, *jaṉam.*
perceive, v., *kāṇu ; aṟi.*
perception, *terind'aṟidal.*
perfection, *çampūraṇam.*
peril, *aradi, ābattu, mōçam.*
period, *kālam.*
perish, *aṟi ; nāça-p-paḍu.*
perjury, *poyyāṇäi.*
permanent, *niläimäiyāṉa.*
permission, *uttaravu, viḍäi.*
permit, n., *uttaravuççīṭṭu ;* v., *oṭṭu, viḍu.*
perseverance, *viḍāmuyaṟci.*
person, *āḷ ; peyar.*
perspiration, *vērväi.*
persuade, *iṇakkappaḍuttu, çammadappaḍuttu.*
pestle, *ulakkäi.*
petition, *arji; maṉu, viṇṇappam.*
phial, *kuppi.*
pick (peck), v., *kottu, piḍuṅgu ;* (choose) *terind'eḍu.*
piece, *tuṇḍu.*
pierce, *kuttu.*
pile (heap), n., *kuviyal;* (stake) *pālan-tāṅgi.*
pile up, v., *aḍukku.*
pillar, *tūṇ.*
pin, *kuṇḍūçi.*
pincers, *iḍukki.*
pinch, v., *kiḷḷu.*
pipe (tube), *kuḻal.*
pipe (tobacco-), *çuṅgāṉ.*
pistol, *käi veḍi.*
pit, *kuḻi, kiḍaṅgu.*
pitch (tar), *kīl.*
pity, n., *paridābam.*
place, *iḍam.*
place, v., *väi ; pōḍu.*
plaintiff, *vādi ; vaḻakkāḷi.*
plan (method), *ōḻuṅgu, upāyam.*
plane, *cīvuḷi.*
plane, v., *çīvu, iḻäi.*
plant, v., *nāṭṭu ; ūṉṟu.*
plaster, n. (medicine), *paṭṭu, çērväi ;* (mortar) *çāndu.*
plaster, v., *pūçu. pūccu.*
platform, *mēḍäi.*
play, v., *viḷäiyāḍu.*
plead for, *parindu pēçu.*
pleasant, *iṉiya.*
pleasantness, *iṉimäi, iṉbam.*
plenty, *miguḍi ; niṟäivu.*
plough, v., *uḻu ;* n., *kalappäi.*
pluck, v., *paṟi, piḍuṅgu.*
plunge, v., *amiḻndu.*
pocket, *çēppu ; çaṭṭäi-c-cākku.*
pod, *neṟṟu.*
point, n., *nuṉi.*
point out, v., *çuṭṭi-k-kāṭṭu.*
poison, *nañju ; viçam.*
pole, *kambam.*
polish, v., *miṉukku.*
politeness, *mariyādäi, upaçāram.*
poll-tax, *taläivarippaṇam.*
pool, *kuṭṭäi ; taḍāgam.*
population, *kuḍi-jaṉam.*
portion, *paṅgu.*
position, *iḍam.*
positive, *uṟudiyāṉa tīrkkamāṉa.*

possession, *udamäi, urimäi*; (lordship) *ātci*.
post (mail), *tapāl*.
post (pillar), *tūṇ*; *kāl*.
post (letters, &c.), v., *tapālil* [*pōḍu*.
postpone, *kaḍattu*.
pot, *kalam, pāṉäi*; *kōppäi*.
potter, *kuçavaṉ*.
pouch, *çākku*; *pai*.
pound (weight), *irāttal*.
pound, v., *kuttu*; *iḍi*.
pour, *vār*.
poverty, *tarittiram*; *vaṟumäi*.
powder, *tūḷ*, *poḍi*.
power, *pelaṉ*; *vallamäi*.
practice, *appiyāçam*; *payiṯci*.
practise, v., *appiyāçam paṇṇu*.
praise, n., *pugaṟci*; *tuti*.
praise, v., *pugaṟu*.
prayer, n., *çebam, pirārttaṉäi*.
preach, *piraçaṅgi*.
precious, *arumäiyāṉa*.
prefer, *terindu koḷ*.
preparation, *āyattam, ettaṉam*.
prepare, *āyattam paṇṇu*.
presence, *mugadā*; *muṉ*.
present (now), *nigaṟugiṟa*, *naḍakkiṟa*. [*āçar*.
present (being), *muṉ irukkiṟa*;
present (gift), *vegumāṉam*; *çantōsham*.
present, v., *koḍu, oppuvi*.
preserve, v., *kāppāṯṯu*.
press (wine-, &c.), *ālāi*.
press, v., *amukku*; *nerukku*.
press out (by hand), v., *piṟi*, *adukku*.
pretend, *pāvaṉäi kāṭṭu*; *pāçāṅgu paṇṇu*.
prevent, *taḍu*; *maṟi*.
previous, *mundiṉa*.

prey, *iräi*.
price, *viläi*.
prick, v., *kuttu*; *tai*.
prickly, *muḷḷuḷḷa*.
pride, *āṅgāram, perumäi*.
prince, *irāja-kumāraṉ*.
princess, *irāja-kumāratti*.
principal, a., *piradāṉa*; (of money), *mudal*.
print, v., *accaḍi*.
prison, *kāvaṯkūḍam*.
prisoner, *kaidi, maṟiyaṯkāraṉ*.
private, *irahaçiya*.
prize, *pandayam, oṭṭam*.
proceed, *naḍa, puṟappaḍu*.
proceeds, *varumāṉam*.
produce, n., *palaṉ*; *viḷäiccal*.
produce, v., *palaṉ koḍu*; *viḷäi*.
product, *palaṉ*; *viḷäivu*.
profession, *vēläi, uttiyōgam*.
profit, n., *ilābam*; v., *pali*.
promise, n., *vākkuttattam*.
promise, v., *vākkuttattam çey*.
pronounce, *uccari*.
proof, *attāṭci*; *uruçu*.
prop, *muṭṭu*.
proper, *tagudiyāṉa*.
property, *uḍäimäi*; *āsti*.
proportion, *piramāṇam, aḷavu*
proprietor, *uḍäiyavaṉ*.
prosecute, *toḍar*.
prosper, *çitti, vāṟu*.
protect, *kāppāṯṯu*.
protection, *pālaṉam, kāppu*.
prove, *oppi*; *meyppi*.
provide, *çambādi, çēgari*.
province, *nāḍu*.
provoke, *kōbamūṭṭu*.
prune, *naṟukku, kavāttu çey*.
pruning-knife, *kavāttuk katti*.
public, *piraçittamāṉa*.

publish, *arivi, piraçittam pannu.*
pull, v., *iru;* n., *iruppu.*
pulley, *kappi.*
pulp, *çulāi; taçāi.*
pulse, n., *nādi.*
punctual, *nēran-tavarāda.*
punish, *tandi.*
pupil, *çīshan, mānākkan.*
purchase, v., *vilāikku vāngu.*
push, v., *tallu.*
put, *idu, vai; pōdu.*
putrid, *arugalāna.*
putty, *makku; patti.*

Quality, *gunam.*
quantity, *alavu.*
quarrel, n., *çandāi; vākkuvādam.*
quarter (¼), *kāl, kālvāçi;* (direction) *diçāi.*
queen, *irājātti, irājastirī.*
quench, *anāi, avi.*
quench thirst, *dāhan tīr.*
question, v., *kēl;* n., *kēlvi.*
quick, *çīkkiramāna.*
quickly, *çīkkiramāy; çuruk-kāy.*
quietness, *amāidi.*
quill, *iragu.*
quite, *muttilum.*

Rail, *kirādi.*
rain-coat, *marāi-c-cattāi.*
rainy season, *mārikālam.*
raise, *tūkku; ēttu.*
rake (tool), *kuppāi vāri.*
rank, n. (order), *variçāi, andastu;* (dignity) *mēnmāi.*
rap, v., *tattu.*
rapid, *virāivāna.*
rasp (file), n., *aram.*
rasp, v., *arāvu.*
rate (ratio), *vīdam, taram.*
raw, *paccāiyāna.*
razor, *çavarakkatti.*
reach, v., *ettu.*
read, *vāci; padi.*
readiness, *āyattam.*
real, *ulla, meyyāna.*
reap, *aru; ari.*
rear, v., *valar.*
reason, *yutti; mugāndiram.*
receipt (note), *pattuccittu, iraçīttu.*
receive, *ēttukkol; pattu; vāngu.*
reckon, *kanakk'idu, ennu.*
recognise, *ari.*
recover (get back), *tirumba adāi.*
recover (from illness), *çugappadu.*
rectify, *çarippaduttu; tiruttu.*
redeem, *mīttu-k-kol.*
Redeemer, *mītpar.*
reduce, *kurāi.*
reed, *nānal.*
refresh one's-self, *muçippāttu.*
refuse, v., *maru;* n., *kariru.*
register, n., *attavanāi, dāppu.*
regret, n., *manastābam;* v. *tukki.*
regular, *orungāna.*
regulate, *tittappaduttu.*
reject, *tallu.*
relate, *çollu; vivari.*
relationship, *uravu.*
release, v., *viduvi.*
relieve, *udavu.*
remain, *tangu; nilāi; tari.*
remainder, *miccam; mīdi.*
remember, *nināivu kūr.*
remove, *eduttu-p-pōdu; peyar.*
renew, *puduppi.*
rent, n., *vādagāi.*
rent, v., *vādagāikku edu.*
repair, v., *parudu pār.*

report (inform), v., *arivi; terivi*; n., *kēlvi, arikkäi.*
resign, *oppukkodu; vittuvidu.*
resin, *kungiliyam.*
resolve, v., *tīrmāni*, [*nu.*
respect, v., *madi; kanam-pan-*
respect (homage), n., *mariyādai, vanakkam.*
rest, *iläippārudal.*
rest, v., *iläippāru; ōy.*
restore, *tirumba-k-kodu.*
restrain, *adakku; tadu.*
result, n., *palan; mudivu*
retain, *vaittukkol,*
retire, *vilagu, pinnidu.*
return, v., *tirumbu.*
reveal, *velippaduttu.*
revenue, *varumānam.*
reverence, n., *vanakkam, vandanam*; v., *madi, vanangu.*
reward, n., *palan, vegumadi.*
ride, v., *kudirāi ērippō*; n., *çavāri.*
ridge (of a house), *mugadu*; (of a field) *varambu*; (of a hill) *ucçi.*
right (lawful, correct), *niyāyamāna; çariyāna.*
right (correctness), *çari, nīti.*
right (side), *valam.*
ring (for finger), *mōdiram.*
— (circle), *vattam.*
— (the bell), v., *mani-y-adi.*
ripe, *parutta.*
rise, v., *erumbu.* [*yāni.*
rivet, v., *kadāvu*; n., *kadäi-*
roam, *tiri.*
roar, v., *iräi; kereci; murangu.*
rob, *tirudu, kollāiyidu.*
robbery, *kollāi.*
rod, *milāru, kōl; kambu.*

roll (scroll), n., *çurul.*
roll, v.intr., *puralu, urulu*; tr., *uruttu, çuruttu.*
root, *kirangu; vēr.*
rope, *kayiru.*
rough, *muradāna.* [*yāna.*
round, a., *rattamāna; undäi-*
round, prep., *çutti; çūra.*
rouse, v.tr., *eruppu; tūndu*, intr., *erumbu.*
row, v., *tandu vali.*
row (line), n., *niräi; variçäi.*
royal, *irājarīgamāna.*
rub, v.tr., *tudäi, tēy*; intr., *urāñju.*
rude, *tadinamāna; murattu.*
rug, *kambali; çūl.* [*ari.*
ruin, n., *arivu, kēdu*; v. *kedu,*
rule (as foot-rule), *kōl.*
rule (regulation), *orungu, çattam, vidi.*
rule, v., *adigārañ çey; ālu.*
ruler (governor), *āndavan, adipati*; (instrument) *rūlkambu.*
rumour, *ōmal, pēççu.*
run, v., *ōdu.*
rupee, *rūbāy.*
rush, v., *pāy.*
rust, n., *turu.*

Sack, *çākku; pai.*
sackcloth, *irattu.*
sacred, *tiru; tivviya.*
sacrifice, *pali.*
sadness, *tukkam; tuyaram.*
safe, a., *pattiramāna; çugamā-*
saffron, *mañjal.* [*na.*
sailor, *kappatkāran.*
salary, *çambalam.*
sale, *vitpanäi.*

saleable, *viṟkattakka.*
salt, adj., *uppāṉa.*
salt-pan, *aḷam.*
salutation, *vandaṉam, upaçā-*
salvation, *iratcippu.* [*ram.*
same, *orē.*
sample, *mustar, mādiri.*
sandal-wood, *çandaṉa-maram.*
sandals, *çeruppu.*
sap, *çāram.*
satisfaction, *tirutti.*
savage, a., *koḍiya.*
save, *iratci.*
saviour, *irtcagar.*
saw, n., *vāḷ*; v., *vāḷāl ari.*
sawyer, *vāṭ-kāraṉ.*
say, *çol*; *eṉ.*
scales, *tarāçu.*
scarcity, *kuṟäiccal.*
scatter, v., *çidaṟu.*
school, *paḷḷikkūḍam.*
science, *çāstiram, kalvi.*
scissors, *kattarikkōl.*
scold, v., *kōbittu-p-pēçu; kaṇḍi.*
scorpion, *tēḷ.*
scrape, *çuranḍu.*
scratch, v., *kīṟu, çoṟi.*
scream, n., *kadaṟugäi;* v., *vīr-*
screw, *tirugāṇi.* [*iḍu.*
screw, v., *tirugāṇi yiḍu; mu-ṟukku.*
scrub, v., *tēy, tudäi.*
sculpture, *çittaravittäi.*
scurvy, *çoṟi karappaṉ.*
scythe, *viccarivāḷ.*
search, v., *tēḍu; ārāy, viçāri;* n., *çōdaṉäi.*
secret, n., *irayaçiyam.*
section, *paṅgu, pirivu.*
security, *piṇäi, jāmīṉ.*
see, *pār.*

seed, *vittu; vidäi; koṭṭäi.*
seedling, *kaṉṟu, nāṯṯu.*
seem, *tōṉṟu.*
seize, *piḍi; paṟi.*
seldom, adv., *aridāy.*
select, v., *terind'eḍu.*
self, *tāṉ.*
sell, *vil.*
send, *aṉuppu.*
sense, *butti.* [*vaṯṯa*
senseless, *buttiyillāda; uṇar-*
sensible, *buttiyuḷḷa.*
sentence (decision), *tīrppu.*
— (gramm.), *vākkiyam.*
separate, adj., *taṉitta; vev-vēṟāṉa.*
separate, v., *piri.*
set (place), v., *vai;* (plant) *nāṭṭu;* (as the sun) *astami.*
set out, *puṟappaḍu.*
set down, *iṟakki viḍu.*
settle, v.tr., *tīrttu-p-pōḍu.*
severe, *kadiṉamāṉa.*
sew, *tai.*
shadow, *niṟal.*
shake, *açäi; udaṟu.*
shallow, a., *āṟamaṯṯa;* n.,
shame, *vetkam.* [*kaḷam*
shape, *vaḍivu; uruvam.*
share, n., *paṅgu, pāgam.*
sharp, *kūrmäiyāṉa.*
shave, *çavaram paṇṇu.*
she, *avaḷ.*
shed, v., *cindu, çori.*
shed, n., *kuḍiçäi, çāyäi.*
sheet, *tuppaṭṭi.*
shelf, *taṭṭu.*
shell, *çippi; ōḍu, çaṅgu.*
shelter, v.tr., *oḍukku;* n., *tañ-*
shoe-lace, *çappāttu vār.* [*jam.*
shoot (with gun), *veḍi vai.*

shop, *kaḍäi.*
short, *kuṭṭäiyāṉa; kiṭṭiṉa.*
shout, v., *çattam pōḍu, ārp-pari.*
show, v., *kāṭṭu.*
shrink, *çuruṅgu.*
shut, *aḍäi; çāttu.*
sickle, *arivāḷ.*
sickness, *viyādi; nōvu.*
side, *pakkam;* (of body) *vilā.*
sieve, *çallaḍäi; çulagu; muṟam.*
sift, *teḷḷu; çali.*
sight, *pārväi.*
sign, n., *aḍäiyāḷam.*
sign, v., *kaiyoppam vai.*
silence, *mauṉam*
similarity, *oppu, çamāṉam.*
simple, *pēḍäimäiyāṉa.*
sin, *pāvam.*
since, adv., *adumudal; toṭṭu, paḍiyāl.*
sincere, *uṇmäiyuḷḷa.*
sing, *pāḍu.*
single, *oṟṟäiyāṉa.*
sink, v., *amiṟ; amiṟttu.*
sir, *aiyā.*
sit down, *uṭkāru.*
site, *iḍam.*
size, *aḷavu.*
skill, *çāmārttiyam.*
slab, *kal-tagaḍu, palagäi.*
slacken, *negiṟ.*
slavery, *aḍimäi.*
sledge-hammer, *çammaṭṭi.*
sleep, *tūkkam; uṟakkam.*
sleep, v., *tūṅgu; nittiräi çey; uṟaṅgu.*
slender, *melivāṉa.*
slice, v., *çīvu.*
slide, v.tr., *çari;* intr., *naṟuvu.*
slip, v., *tavaṟu;* n., *piçagu, tappu.*
slit, *kīṟu.*
slow, *tāmadamāṉa.*
slowly, *meduvāy.*
sluice, *taṇṇīr-k-kadavu.*
small, *çiṉṉa.*
small-pox, *ammäi.*
smash, v., *neri; noṟukku.*
smell, v., *mō, maṇa;* n., *maṇam, gandam.*
smoke (a cigar), v., *çuruṭṭu-k-kuḍi.*
smoothness, *oppam.*
snare, n., *kaṇṇi.*
snipe, *uḷḷāṉ.*
so, *appaḍi; ippaḍi.*
soak, v.intr., *ūṟu.*
soak, v.tr.., *ūṟa vai; tōy.*
sober, *veṟiyillāda, telivāṉa.*
soft, *meduvāṉa, mirudu.*
soil, v., *kaṟäippaḍuttu.*
soldier, *pōrççēvagaṉ.*
solitary, *taṉimäiyāṉa.*
some, *cila; koñja.*
somebody, *yārāvadu, yārō oruvaṉ*
somehow, *eppaḍiyō.*
something, *ēdō.*
sometimes, adv., *çila vēḷäi.*
somewhat, adv., *çaṟṟē.*
somewhere, *eṅgēyō.*
song, *pāṭṭu.*
soon, *çīkkiramāy.*
soothe, *āṟṟu.*
sop (soak), v.tr., *tōy, tuväi.*
sorrow, *tukkam; tuṉbam.*
sound, n., *çattam; ōçai.*
sour, *puḷippāṉa.*
source (of a river), *ūṟṟu.*
south, n., *teṟku.*
south wind, *teṉṟal.*
south-west monsoon, *muṉ-mārikālam.*
sow, v., *vidäi.*

space, *idam; veli.*
span, *jāṇ; çāṇ-alavu.*
speak, *pēçu; çollu.*
spear, *īṭṭi.*
special, *viçēçamāṉa.*
spectacles, *mūkkukkaṇṇāḍi.*
speed, *viräivu.*
spend, v., *çelavari.*
spill, v., *çindu.*
spin, v., *nūṉūl.*
spirits (alcohol), *çārāyam.*
split, v., *pila.*
spoil, v., *keḍu; ari;* n., (plunder) *koḷḷäi.*
sport (jesting), *pagaḍi, kēli.*
spot, *puḷḷi.*
spout, n., *pīli.*
spread, v.intr., *parambu;* tr., *parappu; viri.*
spring (of water), *ūṯṯu;* (trap) *vicäi.*
spring (forth), v., *ūṟu;* (leap) *pāy.*
sprinkle, *tūvu, teḷi.*
sprout, n., *muḷäi; tuḷir.*
square, n., *çaturam.*
squirrel, *aṇil.*
stable, n., *kudirāi-lāyam.*
stain, n., *karäi, māçu.*
stain, v., *karäppaduttu.*
stake, n., *vaçi, kaḷtuttari.*
stamp (trample), v., *midi;* (imprint) *padi.*
stand (stop), *nil;* (— erect), *nimir.*
start (set out), v., *puṟappaḍu.*
state, v., *çol; vivari.*
state (condition), n., *niläimäi, taṉmäi.*
statue, *pāvāi, çilāi.*
stay, v.intr., *taṅgu;* tr., *niṟuttu.*
steal, *kaḷavu çey.*

steam, n., *nīrāvi;* v., *pugäi.*
steep, a., *çeṅguttāṉa;* v., *ūṭṭu, tōy.*
stem (stalk), *kāmbu; taṇḍu.*
steps, *paḍi.*
sticky, *paçäiyāṉa.*
stiff, *viṟäitta; vaḷäiyāda.*
still, adv., *iṉṉam.*
stillness, *amäidi, māvuṉam.*
sting, n., *koḍukku;* v., *koṭṭu.*
stir, v.tr., *kalakku, tūṇḍu;* intr., *açäi.*
stirrup, *aṅgapaḍi.*
stock (of tree), *aḍi maram.*
stop, v.intr., *nil, tari;* tr., *niṟuttu, taḍu;* n., *taḍäi, aḍäippu.*
store-room, *kiḍaṅgu.*
story, *taṭṭu; mettäi.*
story (tale), *kadäi.*
stout, a., *parutta; pushṭiyuḷḷa.*
straight, *nērāṉa.*
strange, *aṉṉiya; navamāṉa.*
strap, *kaccu; vār.*
street, *vīdi, teru.*
strength, *çatti, vallamäi.*
stretch, v., *nīṭṭu; viri; nīḷu.*
strict, *kaṇḍippāṉa.*
strike, *aḍi; aṟäi.*
string, n., *nūl; kayiṟu.*
strip, v., *ellām piḍuṅgu; uri.*
strong, *palamuḷḷa, valla, valiya*
struggle (wrestle), v., *malluk-kaṭṭu.*
stumble, *iḍaṟu, tuvaṟu.*
stupid, *mūḍamāṉa.*
subject, n., *poruḷ, kāriyam;* a., *kīṟppaṭṭa, aḍaṅgiya.*
subdue, *kīṟppaduttu, aḍakku.*
submit, *aḍaṅgu.*
substance, *poruḷ; vastu.*

subtract, *kaṛi.*
succeed (prosper), *çitti;* (follow) *piṉtoḍar.*
success, *vāyppu, çitti.*
such, *appaḍippaṭṭa.*
suddenly, *çaḍudiyāy.*
suffer, *paḍu; çagi.*
sufficient, *tiruttiyāṉa.*
sugar-cane, *karumbu.*
suitable, *tagudiyāṉa.*
sultry, *puṛukkamāṉa.*
sum, *togäi.*
summons, *kaṭṭaḷäi, çittāçi.*
sunshine, *veyil.*
superintendent, *periya turäi; adigāri.*
superior, a., *mēlāṉa.*
superior, n., *mēlāṉavaṉ.*
support, n., *tāṅgi; ādaravu.*
support, v., *tāṅgu; ādari.*
suppose, *niṉäi, eṉṉu.*
sure, *niççayamāṉa.*
surprise, n., *accariyam.*
surround, *çuṭṭu, valäi.*
survey (land), *nilām-aḷa;* (look over) *nōkku.*
suspect, *çandēgappaḍu.*
swarm, n., *tiraḷ, kūṭṭam.*
swarm, v., *tiraḷu, moy.*
sweep, v., *perukku; kūṭṭu.*
sweeper, *tōṭṭi,* (fem.) *tōṭṭicci.*
sweet, *tittippāṉa, iṉiya.*
swell, v., *vīṅgu; perugu; adai.*
swim, *nīndu.*
sword, *paṭṭayam, vāḷ.*
sympathy, *paridābam.*
symptom, *kuri.*
system, *oṛuṅgu; kiramam.*

Tail, *vāl.*
take, *eḍu; vāṅgu.*
talk, v., *pēçu; çambāshi.*
tall, *neḍiya neṭṭäiyāṉa.*
tamarind, *puḷi.*
tame, *çāduvāṉa.*
tank, *kuḷam.*
tape, *nāḍā.*
tapioca, *ēṛiläik-kiṛaṅgu mā.*
tar, *kīl; tār.*
target, *ilakku.*
task, *kuṟitta vēläi.*
taste, n., *uruçi; çuväi.*
tax, n., *çuṅgam; vari; tīrväi.*
tea (leaf), *tēyiläi.*
teach, *pōdi; paḍippi.*
teacher, n., *uvātti; pōdagar.*
teak, *tēkku-maram.*
teal, *çiṟagi.*
tear (drop), *kaṇṇīr.*
tear (rend), v., *kiṛi; pīṟu.*
tell, *çol; aṟivi.*
temper (disposition), *guṇam.*
temperance, *iccäi-y-aḍakkam.*
temple, *kōvil.*
tempt, *çōdi.*
temptation, *çōdaṉäi.*
tenant, *kuḍi, puṟakkuḍi.*
tend (cattle), v., *āḍu māḍu mēy.*
tender (young), *iḷa; iḷaçaṉa.*
tent, *kūḍāram.*
term, *tavaṇäi.*
terms, *oppanda vivaraṅgaḷ.*
than, *pārkkilum.*
that, pron., *adu;* a., *anda.*
that, conj., *eṉṟu, eṉa.*
thatch, n., *pullu;* v., *vēy, mēy.*
theft, *kaḷavu; tiruṭṭu.*
then, *apporudu, appōdu; aṉṟu.*
thence, *adilirundu; adumudal.*
there, *aṅgē; avviḍattil.*
therefore, *āgäiyāl.*

thick, *kaṉatta;* (dense) *aḍarnda.*
thief, *kaḷavāḷi; tiruḍaṉ.*
thigh, *toḍäi.*
thin, *melliya; olli.*
thing, *vastu, poruḷ; kāriyam.*
think, *niṉäi;* (deliberate), *ālōçi.*
thirst, n., *tāgam.*
this, pron., *idu;* a., *inda.*
thorn, *muḷ.*
thorough, *tiṭṭamāṉa.*
thoroughly, *tīrkkamāy; muṯṯa.*
thou, *nī.*
thought, *niṉäivu; çintaṉäi.*
thread, *nūl.*
threaten, *payam uṟuttu.*
threshing floor, *kaḷam.*
thrive, *çeṟi, çēmamāy iru.*
throne, *çimmāçaṉam.*
through, *ūḍē; uruva.*
throughout, *eṅgum; muṟudum.*
throw, *eṟi.*
thrust, *taḷḷu; neṭṭu.*
thus, *ippaḍi; indavagäiyil.*
thyself, *nī tāṉē.*
tie, v., *kaṭṭu; muḍi.*
tile, *ōḍu.*
till (until), *varäikkum; maṭṭum.*
tillage, *uṟavu.*
timber, *maram.*
time, *kālam.*
timid, *kōṟäiyuḷḷa.*
tire (become tired), *iḷaittup*
title (rank), *paṭṭap-pēr.* [*pō.*
together, *kūḍa; orumikka.*
toll (duty), *āyam, çuṅgam.*
tom-tom, *paṟäi.*
too, *kūḍa; um.*
tool, *karuvi; āyudam.*
top, *meṟpakkam.*

torch, *tīvaṭṭi.*
toss, v., *eṟi; aläi.*
total, n., *togäi.*
touch, v., *toḍu.*
tough, *uramuḷḷa.*
toward, *nērāga.*
tower, *gōpuram, turukkam.*
town, *paṭṭaṇam.*
trace, n., *çuvaḍu, vaṟi-k-kuṟi.*
trace, v., *piṉ toḍar.*
track, n., *taḍam; çuvaḍu; kāṭṭup pādäi.*
train, v., *paṟakku, vaçakku,*
trample, *midi.* [*paḍippi.*
transfer, v., *koḍuttu viḍu, çāṭṭu.*
translate, *tiruppu.*
transplant, *peyarttu naḍu.*
transport, v., *peyar.*
trap, *poṟi.*
travel, v., *pirayāṇam paṇṇu, payaṇam pō.*
tray, *taṭṭu.*
treachery, *turōgam.*
tree, *maram.*
tremble, v., *adir, naḍuṅgu.*
trench, *vāykkāl, agaṟ.*
trespass, v., *elläi kaḍa, tavaṟu.*
trial (examination), *viçāraṇäi; çōdaṉäi.*
triangle, *mukkōṇam.*
tribe, *jāti, gottiram.*
tribute, *iṟäi, kappam.* [*yam.*
trifle, n., *çoṟpam; aṟpakkāri-*
trigger, *viçäi; poṟuppu.*
troop, n., *paḍai, çēṉäi.*
trouble, n., *çaṅgaḍam; tonda-*
trough, *toṭṭi; pattal.* [*ravu.*
trowel, *karaṇäi.*
trumpet, *ekkāḷam, tāṟäi.*
trunk (of a tree), *aḍimaram;* (of elephant) *tumbikkäi.*

trust, *nambikkäi.*
trust, v., *nambu.*
truth, *mey.*
try, v.intr., *pirayāçap-paḍu;* tr., *parītci, çōdi.*
tube, *kuṛal.*
tune, *irāgam.*
turban, *taläippā.* [*tiruppu.*
turn, v.intr., *tirumbu;* tr.,
tusk, *kombu, dantam.*
twins, *iraṭṭäippiḷḷäigaḷ.*
twine (string), *nūḻ kayiṟu.*
twist, v., *tiri; muṟukku.*
twofold, a., *irumaḍaṅgāṉa.*
type (print.), *accu.*

Ugly, *avalaṭcaṇamāṉa.*
unable, *kūḍāda; iyalāda.*
uncommon, *vaṛaṅgāda; apūrvamāṉa.*
uncover, *mūḍal eḍu; tiṟa.*
under, *kīṛē.*
undergo, *paḍu.* [*kīṛāṉa.*
underground, a., *pūmikkuk-*
understand, *aṟi; vilaṅgu; teri.*
undertake, *ēṟpaḍu; kaiyiḍu.*
underwood, *ciṟu kāḍu.*
undo, *aviṛ.*
undress, *uḍuppuk-kaṛaṭṭu.*
undulating, *mēḍu-paḷḷamāṉa.*
unequal, *vittiyāçamāṉa.*
uneven, *karaḍu-muraḍāṉa.*
unfair, *aniyāyamāṉa.*
unfold, *viri, tiṟa.*
unfortunate, *çitti peṟāda.*
unfit, *āgāda; tagāda.*
unfruitful, *kaṉi koḍāda.*
ungrateful, *naṉṟi maṟanda.*
union, *aikkiyam.* [*poruttu, içäi.*
unite, v.intr., *porundu;* tr.,
universal, *eṅgum uḷḷa.*

unjust, *anītiyuḷḷa.* [*ṉam.*
unkindness, *abayāram, kaḍi-*
unknown, *aṟiyāda.*
unlawful, *nītikku virōdamāṉa.*
unlike, *ottirāda.* [*māṉa.*
unnatural, *iyalbukku virōda-*
unpack, v., *tiṟand'iḍu; aviṛ.*
unroll, *viri.*
unsaddle, *çēṉaṅ-kaṛaṭṭu.*
unsafe, *pattiram-illāda.*
unscrew, *tirugāṇi kaṛaṭṭu.*
unusual, *vaṛakkam illāda.*
up, adv., *uyara; mēlē.*
upon, *mēlē.*
upper, *mēlāṉa.*
upside down, *kīṛadu mēla-*
urge, *ēvu.* [*dāga.*
usage, *vaṛakkam.*
use, v., *vaṛaṅgu, kaiyāḷu,*
useful, *pirayōjaṉam-uḷḷa.*
utmost, *kaḍaiçiyāṉa.*
utmost, n., *iyaṉṟa-maṭṭum.*
utter, v., *çol.*
utterly, *muṭṭum.*

Vacancy, *iḍäiveḷi; kāli.*
vain, *vīṇāṉa.*
value, n., *viläi; kirayam.*
vanish, *maṟäi.*
vapour, *āvi, kāṉal.*
various, *nāṉāvida.*
vast, *viçālamāṉa.*
vehicle, *banḍi, vāhaṉam.*
veil, *mukkāḍu.*
vein, *narambu.*
venom, *visham.*
ventilate, *tūṭṭu.*
verandah, *viṟāndā.*
verdict, *tīrppu.*
verdure, *paçumäi.*
verse, *çulōgam; kavi.*

very, *migavum ; mettu.*
vessel, *pāttiram;* (ship) *kappal*
vex, *varuttap-paduttu.* [*rāvi.*
vice (blacksmith's), *piditti-*
view, n., *tōttam, kātci.*
vile, *irivāna, pollāda.*
violence, *balavantam ; kodu-*
virtue, *aram ; çatkunam.* [*māi.*
visit, v., *çandi.*
vivid, *adigap-piragāçamāna.*
voice, *çattam ; kural.* [v., *nēr.*
vow, n., *poruttanāi ; nērcci ;*

Wager, *ottam, pandāiyam*
wages, *kūli, çambalam.*
waist, *idāi, arāi.*
wait, v., *kātt'iru.*
wake, v.intr., *viri, erumbu.*
wake, v.tr., *eruppu.*
walk, v., *nada* ; n., *nadāi.*
wall, *çuvar.*
wander (stray), *alāi.* [n., *tēvāi.*
want, v., *tēvāiyāy iru; vēndum;*
war, *yuttam ; çandāi.*
warehouse, *panda-çālāi.*
warm, *analulla.*
warm, v., *kāyccu; kāy.* [*lāi*
warrant, n., *vārāndu, katta-*
wash, v.tr., *karuvu ;* intr.,
karāi, karuvu.
washerman, *vannān.*
wasp, *kulavi.*
waste, v., *vīnāyccelavari ;* a.,
pār. [(guard), *kāval.*
watch (timepiece), *gadiyāram;*
watch, v., *kāvatkā ; viri.*
watchman, *kāvatkāran.*
water, v., *nīrp-pāyccu.*
water-pot, *kudam.* [*yantiram.*
water-wheel, *nīr-rōdāi ; nīr-*
wax, *arakku ; merugu.*

way (road), *vari, āru ;* (manner), *vidam, vagāi.*
weak, *balavīna.* [*tēy.*
wear, v.tr., *udutti-k-kol ;* intr.,
weave, *ney.*
wedge, n., *āppu.*
weed mattock, *pul-vetti.*
weep, v., *kannīr-vidu ; aru.*
weigh, v., *niru.*
weight, *nirāi ; pāram.*
well, a., *nanrāy.*
west, n., *mētku.* [v., *nanāi.*
wet, a., *īramāna, nanāinda ;*
what, pron., *enna ; edu.*
when, *eppōdu.*
whence, *eṅgirundu.*
whenever, *epporudānālum.*
where, *eṅge ; evvidattil.*
wherever, *eṅgēyāgilum.*
which, pron., *yādu ; edu.*
while, *porudu.*
whisper, v., *kādukkul çollu.*
whistle, n., *çīrkkāi ;* v., *çīrk-*
kāi-vidu.
who, pron., *ār ; yār, evan.*
whoever, *yārānālum.*
whole, n., *ellām ; murumāi.*
wholly, *murudumāy ; mutti-*
why, *ēn, ennattukku.* [*lum.*
wick, *tiri.*
wicked, *pollāda.*
wide, *agalamāna ; viçālamā-*
widow, *kaim-pen.* [*na*
widower, *tāram irandavan.*
width, *agalam.*
wild, *kāttu ; dushta, kādāna.*
will (mind), n., *çittam; manam.*
win, *keli, vel.* [*tūttu, pudai.*
winnow, *çulagu, muram ;* v.,
wipe, *tudāi.*
wire, *kambi.*

wisdom, *ñāṉam.*
wish, v., *virumbu.*
with, *kūḍa.*
within, *uḷ; uḷḷē.*
without, *illāmal; oṟiya; iṉṟi.*
witness (person), *çāṭcik-kāraṉ.*
witness, v., *çāṭci çollu; pār.*
woodcutter, *kāḍu-veṭṭi.*
word, *çol, vārttäi.*
work, n., *vēläi;* v., *vēläi çey.*
worth, n., *arumäi, mēṉmäi.*
worthy, *pāttiramāṉa; tagudiyāṉa.*
wound, n., *kāyam.*
wrap, v., *çuṯṯu; pōr; uḍuttu.*
wring, v., *piḻi.*
writ, *çādaṉam.*
write, *eḻudu.*
wrong, a., *tappidamāṉa; kuṯṯamuḷḷa.*
wrong, n., *tīṅgu, tappidam.*

Yam, *kiḻaṅgu.*
yard (courtyard), *muṯṯam;* (measure) *yāru, gajam.*
yawn, *koṭṭāvi viḍu.*
yet, *āṉālum; iṉṉam.*
yield, v., *koḍu; viläi; iṇaṅgu.*
yonder, *avviḍattil.*
young, a., *iḷäiya.*
young (of animals), n., *kuṭṭi; kuñju; kaṉṟu.*

MONEY, WEIGHTS & MEASURES.

TAMIL-ENGLISH VALUES.

		£	s	d
1 anna (6¼ centièmes)	=			1
½ rupee (8 annas)	=			8
12 annas (75 c.)	=		1	0
1 rupee (16 a. or 100 c.)	=		1	4
3 rupees	=		4	0
4 „	=		5	4
5 „	=		6	8
7 „	=		9	4
8 „	=		10	8
10 „	=		13	4
15 „	=	1	0	0
50 „	=	3	6	8
100 „	=	6	13	4
1,000 rupees ...	=	66	13	4
100,000 „ (1 lac)	=	6,666	13	4

ENGLISH-TAMIL VALUES.

£	s	d		
		1	=	1 anna (6¼c.)
		4	=	4 annas (25c.)
		6	=	6 „ (37½c.)
	1	0	=	12 „ (75c.)
	2	0 ...	=	1r. 8a.
	2	6 ...	=	1r. 14a.
	4	0 ...	=	3r. 0a.
	5	0 ...	=	3r. 12a.
	7	0 ...	=	5r. 4a.
	9	0 ...	=	6r. 12a.
	10	0 ...	=	7r. 8a.
1	0	0 ...	=	15r.
10	0	0 ...	=	150r.
100	0	0 ...	=	1,500r.
1,000	0	0 ...	=	15,000r.

TAMIL-AMERICAN VALUES.

1 anna (6¼ centièmes)	=	$0·2
½ rupee (8 annas)	=	0·16
1 „ (16 „)	=	0·33
3 „	=	1·00
5 „	=	1·66
10 „	=	3·33
100 „	=	33·33

AMERICAN-TAMIL VALUES.

$0·1	=	½ anna (3 cents)
0·5	=	2½ annas (15½c.)
0·20	=	10 „ (62½c.)
0·50 ...	=	1r. 9a.
1·00 ...	=	3r. 2a.
10·00 ...	=	31r. 4a.
100·00 ...	=	312r. 8a.

NOTE.—The exchange value of the rupee is subject to slight fluctuation.

TAMIL MONEY.

8 pies (*paiçā*) ...	=	1 thūttū (*tuṭṭu*)
12 pies (4 thūttūs) ...	=	1 anna (*aṇā*) or 1 fanam [(*paṇam*)
16 annas ... ... 100 centièmes (*çatam*)	=	1 rupee (*rūpāy*)

NOTE.—*Centiemes* or *cents* are copper coins used in Ceylon.

WEIGHT. (*Niṟäi.*)

		Troy.	Avoirdupois.
1 mañjāḍi ...		= 3 to 4·15 gr. (about)	
2 mañjāḍis	= 1 fanam (*paṇam*)	= 6 gr.	,,
9 fanams	= 1 pagoda (*varāhaṉ*)	= 54 gr.	,,
10 pagodas	= 1 pollum (*palam*)	= 540 gr.	,,
40 pollums	= 1 viss (*viçäi*)		= 3 lb. 2 oz.
8 viss	= 1 maund (*maṉ*)		= 25 lb.
1 Bengal maund			= 82$\frac{2}{7}$ lb.
20 maunds	= 1 candy (*kaṇḍi*) or bāram ...		= 500 lb. (about)
100 pollums	= 1 tulām (in some places)		
12 tulāms	= 1 podi or bullock-load		

LINEAR MEASURE. (*Nīṭṭal-aḷavu.*)

12 fingers' breadth (*viral kaḍäi*)	=	1 span (*jāṉ*)
2 spans (about 18 inches)	=	1 moolum (*muṟam*) or cubit
2 moolums or 3 feet	=	1 *gajam* (yard)
2 gajams (yards) ...	=	1 *taṇḍam* (fathom)
2000 taṇḍams (fathoms)	=	1 coss (*kōçu* or *kurōçam*) or 2 Indian [miles
4 coss	=	9·09 miles

MEASURE OF CAPACITY. (*Mugattal-aḷavu.*)

8 ollocks (*āṟākku*) or çuṇḍu	=	1 puddy (*paḍi*), *nāṛi*, or *kottu* (about 100 cub. in. capacity)
8 puddies	=	1 marcal (*marakkāl*) or *kuṟuṇi*
5 marcals (according to some)	=	1 parrah (*paṟäi*)
24 seers (*çēr*) ...	=	1 parrah
12 marcals	=	1 kalam
400 marcals	=	1 garce (*karaçäi* or *kariçu*) or 194 c. ft. 768 c. in.

POSTAGE.

The postal rates *from* India (British) and Ceylon to the United Kingdom are as follows: For **Letters**, from India, 1 anna per ½ oz.; from Ceylon, 6 cents per ½ oz. **Postcards**, from India, 1a.; Ceylon, 6 cents. **Newspapers**, from India, ½ anna per 50 grammes; Ceylon, 3 cents for first 50 grammes, and 2 cents per 2 oz. afterwards.

P.O 8.148F